Glass Ceilings and 100-Hour Couples

Classification and Nomenclature

KARINE MOE AND DIANNA SHANDY

Glass Ceilings and 100-Hour Couples

WHAT THE OPT-OUT PHENOMENON CAN TEACH US ABOUT WORK AND FAMILY

THE UNIVERSITY OF GEORGIA PRESS Athens and London

© 2010 by the University of Georgia Press
Athens, Georgia 30602
www.ugapress.org
All rights reserved
Set in Sabon by Graphic Composition, Inc.

Printed digitally in the United States of America

Library of Congress Cataloging-in-Publication Data

Moe, Karine S.
Glass ceilings and 100-hour couples : what the opt-out phenomenon can teach us about work and family / Karine Moe and Dianna Shandy.
xiv, 215 p. ; 22 cm.
Includes bibliographical references and index.
ISBN-13: 978-0-8203-3154-6 (cloth : alk. paper)
ISBN-10: 0-8203-3154-6 (cloth : alk. paper)
ISBN-13: 978-0-8203-3404-2 (pbk. : alk. paper)
ISBN-10: 0-8203-3404-9 (pbk. : alk. paper)
1. Work and family—United States.
2. Working mothers—United States.
3. Stay-at-home mothers—United States.
4. Women—Employment—United States.
5. Dual-career families—United States.
6. Glass ceiling (Employment discrimination)—United States.
I. Shandy, Dianna J. II. Title
HD4904.25.M635 2010
650.1—dc22   2009017227

British Library Cataloging-in-Publication Data available

To our families,
Avery, Halsey, Paul,
Rhetta, Oran, and David

Contents

Prologue

We traded our twenties for doctorates and our thirties for elusive tenure-track jobs. In and amongst school and work, we both married professionals and had kids, albeit on different timelines. An occasional perk of our jobs is that we are eligible for what is known as an academic sabbatical. It's an admittedly generous perk, and on good days we agree that our twenties were a fair swap for these blocks of time away from our ordinary teaching and administrative responsibilities. During these breaks, we embark on research and writing projects, rejuvenate, and try to impose order on the parts of our lives that fall into disarray when we're working full-time, as they are wont to do in households with kids where both parents work. Yet the best part of these sabbaticals is that we have a lot more time to spend at home and with our friends and families. For a little while, we "working moms" get a chance to live more or less like "at-home moms." And this, of course, gives us occasion to reflect on just how whatever it is one has to do usually expands to fill the allotted space, and soon we find ourselves up to our ears in all the many activities that keep at-home moms busy and schools and communities humming along.

It was during one of these at-home-mom impersonation stints that we reflected on what we were getting versus what were we giving up in our choices about career and kids. Snuggling in bed at night with the kids reading stories felt really good. Excavating piles of debris to reveal the tabletop below was a quick high (and we knew there was plenty more where that came from). The oohs and aahs at Thanksgiving dinner for the cornucopia wrought from breadsticks were powerfully and surprisingly gratifying. (Thanks,

Martha!) It's not that we hadn't thought about the career-family equation before, like when we were willing the breast milk on ice in the suitcase to survive the flight home from a business trip, or when we were grading papers at 2 a.m. after getting a sick kid to bed. Yet, somehow, thinking about quitting work while in the throes of the working-mom shuffle was qualitatively different than thinking about returning to work when immersed in full-time motherhood. There's no question that it felt gratifying to be home with the kids and, quite frankly, to live in a far saner, less-hectic environment. Yet even under the drug of domesticity, we knew there was a motivation for why we chose to work outside the home, even on days (and nights) when it was challenging. We just couldn't quite dredge up the reasoning behind the choices we had made. We hung on to the notion that investing a couple of decades in our educations and careers amounted to more than "it seemed like a good idea at the time," even though we were challenged in this on a regular basis by seeing women around us who had chosen to resign from their jobs and stay home.

Over lunch and on walks, we asked ourselves and each other: What was the original impetus for our respective decisions to pursue graduate school and careers? How were we influenced by our grandmother's generation, our mother's generation, our peers, feminism, American notions of individualism and self-reliance? Now that we had "proven" ourselves and even paid back our education loans, what kept us working? (We are admittedly privileged in that, for now anyway, our husbands' incomes could support the family if we tightened our belts and decided to stay home with the children. Although in our research we soon found that for families who do make this decision, this financial threshold is a lot lower than one might think.) How did our experiences of raising our own daughters and sons play into all of this? What did it mean that we, as a baby boomer from Long Island and a Gen X farm girl from Kansas, shared so many of the same cultural understandings about career and children? What were these larger societal messages that transcended our individual life trajectories and had shaped our "choices"? If we spent part of our time as working moms and part as at-home moms, were we acting as some sort of double agents in the mommy wars? And, if so, could our liminal status as working mom/at-home mom yield insights into this complex terrain of women, work, and identity in the twenty-first century? As a labor economist and a cultural anthropologist, we ultimately moved from idle musings to systematic inquiry to considered reflection, and this book is the result of that process.

Acknowledgments

We want to express our deep appreciation to all of the people who helped us to write this book. We thank Derek Krissoff for seeing the potential in our idea and for his enthusiastic and expert guidance, Molly Thompson for excellent copyediting suggestions, and Jon Davies and the rest of the University of Georgia Press team for all their help in bringing the book to print.

We thank our many Macalester College colleagues who provided enormous support and guidance for our research by offering advice, sharing their insights and experience, and serving as sounding boards for our thoughts and arguments: Jack Weatherford, David McCurdy, Sonia Patten, Arjun Guneratne, Sarah West, Terry Boychuk, Barbara Laskin, Dan Balik, Diane Michelfelder, and Kathy Murray. We also are grateful for the support of Kate Abbott, Gabrielle Lawrence, and Helen Warren of the Macalester Development Office. We thank Brad Belbas for helping us to implement our online survey and for technical support. Macalester College supported this project through both a grant and sabbatical leaves, which allowed us time to collaborate and to write.

Many other individuals helped shape this study in important ways. We thank Nora Johnson for excellent assistance with interviewing and transcription. We also are grateful to Macalester students and staff Tara Hottman, Melinda Studer, Joey Dobson, Mark Saldana, Josh Paulson, and Jane Kollasch, who helped with graphics, proofreading, and administrative assistance. Many more Macalester students contributed to this work through their thoughtful classroom engagement with issues raised by this book. We appreciate the input of Michael Paolisso, Ray Hames, and Kathy

Oths of the National Science Foundation Field Methods in Cultural Anthropology Program, who gave us critical feedback on our survey design. Jennifer Keil provided important economic insights. Elrena Evans, Donna Gilleskie, Marianne Ferber, Charlanne Burke, and Susan Rabiner provided insightful comments and helpful suggestions on the manuscript.

Most importantly, we are indebted to the many women and men who took the time to talk with us about the joys, triumphs, and challenges they encountered in raising their families. Many friends, particularly the women in our book club, supported this project in so many ways, especially in listening to us think through our ideas.

Finally, we thank our families for their love and for the patience they showed to us at every stage of writing this book. Dianna acknowledges, with gratitude, the sacrifices her parents, Gary and Joy Shandy, made to let education be such a transformative force in her own coming-of-age story. She is indebted to her husband, David Power, and her children, Rhetta and Oran, for their many kindnesses, their patience, and their support throughout the writing of this book, and always. Karine is deeply grateful for the unwavering support of her parents, Roy and Rigmor Swensen. She thanks her children, Avery and Halsey, who bring joy to the struggle of balancing work and family. And especially, she thanks her husband, Paul, for cheerleading, proofreading, taking on so much of the second shift, and, as always, for being her best friend.

Glass Ceilings and 100-Hour Couples

Introduction

*A woman, just like a man, may have a great
gift for some particular thing. That does
not mean that she must give up the joy of
marrying and having a home and children.*
ELEANOR ROOSEVELT, *It's Up to the Women*, 1933

Eleanor Roosevelt's words still resonate in America today. Her book *It's Up to the Women* was published during a period of economic turbulence that rivals our own. It, like many books today about women and work, was met with great controversy, and her chapter on women and jobs upset people the most. Well into the twenty-first century, our society continues to struggle with how to accommodate women who seek to combine paid work and caring for their children. The contours of the dynamic have shifted substantially, but the central dilemma endures.

In this book, we draw on our backgrounds as social scientists to chart a path through the complexity of how American women frame their relationship with work, and of the political, economic, demographic, social, and cultural forces that shape this relationship in the twenty-first century. In particular, we consider what the decisions women make about work mean to them and to their families. Drawing on hundreds of interviews from around the country, original survey research, and national labor force data, this book combines meaningful statistics and the experiences of real women and their families in order to explore the realities of combining a career with raising children.

The movement of women into the workforce during the last century represented a major demographic shift in American society that transformed the landscape of families and workplaces. When *It's Up to the Women* was published, it was rare for women to hold paid jobs. Today, six in ten women are employed. Together, these women make up almost half of the American labor force. How women respond to the marketplace in terms of supplying or withholding their labor, therefore, has significant implications for the intersection of gender and work, as well as dramatic ramifications for economic growth in America.

For many, women's movement into the labor force is synonymous with societal progress. As the excerpt from Eleanor Roosevelt's book reminds us, it was not that long ago when the idea of women holding paid jobs was radical. Some women today do work because they realize that they benefited from educational opportunities women in their mother's generation never dreamed of having. Other women work because they find their jobs rewarding. Many, many more juggle work and children because their families depend on their income, and this financial imperative is central to any discussion of gender, work, and family.

Given this march of women into the labor force, people were surprised when the new millennium heralded some important and unexpected shifts in women's relationship to work. For example, the labor force participation of college-educated, married mothers of infants fell steeply, from 71 percent in 1997 to 63 percent in 2005.[1] What's more, the full-time labor force participation of married women with professional degrees and children under eighteen fell from nearly two-thirds to just over one-half between 1998 and 2005.[2] Women who left their careers, particularly those who were big earners or who left high-profile positions, garnered the media-generated moniker "opt-out women." This trend was simultaneously trumpeted as a revolution and derided as a myth. In our view, this phenomenon falls somewhere in the middle, neither revolution nor myth. Still, it is an important and very real part of the unfolding story of women and paid work. In this book, we explore what college-educated mothers who leave their jobs can teach us about the intersection of gender, work, and identity in America.

In this way, while this book speaks specifically to the situation of women who are, or who hope to become, mothers, it also is meaningful to those interested in how gender is at work in our society.

Accordingly, this book shifts the nature of the discussion of these so-called opt-out women from one where they are the object of scrutiny to one where their aspirations and struggles serve as a lens through which we can consider much larger societal issues. Often dismissing these individuals as elite women who do not constitute a numerically significant proportion of the population, many fail to recognize the symbolic and real importance of these women's actions and how their walking away from pathbreaking careers reveals flaws in how our society accommodates women who seek to combine jobs and motherhood. "Opting out" is an action taken by a minority of working women. However, their dramatic exit from the labor force is meaningful because it renders visible the dilemmas faced by the many more women who continue to juggle work and home. In this respect, understanding the lives of women who leave their careers to start families or to raise children has much to tell us about the constraints mothers who remain in their jobs face.

At the very least, the experiences of women who leave their jobs to raise families suggest a need for a deeper evaluation of the issues at hand and give rise to a battery of questions: Will history ultimately prove that those who left their hard-won place on the career ladder were bellwether women who presaged the future? Or, will their actions be chalked up to some sort of fin-de-siècle folly? Even if women who left their jobs to raise children do not represent the "everywoman" experience in America, what can be gleaned by examining their lives? At the very least, what do their experiences contribute to the dominant narrative of women's entry into the labor force over time? If no opt-out "revolution" occurred, how do we explain the plunge in full-time labor force participation of highly educated, married women at the turn of the twenty-first century? In what ways do statistics about being "in" or "out" of the labor force obscure the lived experiences of women? Even as our economy strains under the latest crisis and perhaps drives many of these same women who "opted out" back to work, what can be learned from this unusually rich part of the unfolding experience of gender and labor in America? For every woman who "opted out," how many other women made accommodations for family by reducing their hours at work, forgoing a promotion, or choosing job flexibility over potential for professional advancement?

Attuned to issues of identity, the demands of culturally proscribed intensive motherhood, and the importance of using the family, as opposed to just the woman, as a unit of analysis, we argue that in order to make sense of why women are opting out of or ratcheting down their careers, we must first ask why this is happening *now*. We contend that women's relationship with work in our society is situated at the crosscurrents of some significant demographic and societal shifts. Just as women's educational credentials are achieving parity with men's, we find that the higher one climbs the income ladder, the more hours one works. Whereas previous generations saw a surplus of professional men relative to women, the educational gap has closed. Instead of the CEO marrying his secretary or the doctor marrying his nurse, the CEO is marrying the CFO and the doctor is marrying the doctor. And when two professionals marry, this gives rise to something we call the "100-hour couple," or a couple where the husband and wife work extremely long hours for a combined total of well over one hundred hours per week. Add to this the increased demands of parenting measured in something women call "mama time," and we see the perfect storm of social forces culminating in a situation where women are reevaluating their relationship with work in light of family demands.

Our analysis exposes flaws in how our society accommodates women who seek to combine paid work and raising children, with time as a finite resource. Despite the tremendous gains in women's education, jobs, and income over the past decades, their continued struggle to juggle work and home lays bare the pressure our society places on nuclear families, rather than firms or government, to raise the next generation. And children are expensive: the U.S. Department of Agriculture estimates that parents with incomes between $45,800 and $77,100 can expect to spend $204,060 to raise their child from birth to age seventeen.[3] But, this expense pales in comparison to the economic price that mothers pay in terms of reduced labor-market work. As economist Nancy Folbre puts it, Americans expect parents (and especially mothers) to pay these costs because our society views children as pets.[4] Parents chose to have kids, so parents should be responsible for feeding them, caring for them, taking them to the vet (we mean pediatrician). The problem with this way of thinking is that while a dog does not contribute to society at large, children will grow to become productive members of society. Parents who raise the next generation of workers in effect create extraordinary value for society with little to no compensation. Of course, we acknowledge that the reasons for and the rewards gained from being a parent don't fit neatly onto a spreadsheet—but neither do the losses experienced by women who feel forced to choose between family and a career.

This book is sympathetic to the tough circumstances women face in juggling children and career. Rather than viewing women who respond to the pressures of work and home as some aggregate of individuals "choosing" the seemingly irrational option of walking away from hard-won success, it is important to look at these individuals' actions within a wider social context. We suggest that women are motivated to leave or to downsize their careers by a range of factors, including cultural expectations about parenthood, limited available child care options, and the desire to relieve stress for their families and for themselves. Women want to spend time with their children and spouse, and a lack of flexible work options has forced many to choose resigning their jobs altogether or embarking on a "mommy track," which does not allow them to devote time to family for a period of their lives and then resume upward mobility in their careers on a par with their male colleagues who are parents.[5]

Another force that helps to explain women leaving work for home is the existence of social networks. College-educated at-home moms today enjoy the support of other like-minded women who make the same choice. Here, again, the significance of why women are doing this *now* is important to understanding what is taking place. In one at-home mom's words, "I run with a pack of smart women." The result is the formation of social networks of mothers providing a sense of support, occasions for conversation that include but are not limited to domestic matters, and opportunities for their children to play together. Although it may not always be fun to be an ex-attorney who stays home by herself with her kids, it is more appealing to do so when all your friends are doing it, too. The formation of social networks of college-educated at-home moms helps women to maneuver in our society, where occupation is the primary source of one's public social identity.

While elements of being home were alluring to many of the women we interviewed, most women described work-based pressures that also contributed to their rethinking of their relationship with work. The modern workplace makes demands on workers outside of a traditional nine-to-five workday, and these demands often collide with child care arrangements that conform to this schedule. Accordingly, access to child care was a major issue faced by women we interviewed. For some women, the sheer number of hours their jobs expected them and their spouses to work made child care a three-shifts-of-nannies affair. Some of the women we interviewed deemed this unacceptable and, seeing no way to reduce their time at work, quit their jobs entirely.

Most people are well aware of the concept of a glass ceiling, meaning a form of discrimination that limits a woman's advancement at work. Fewer are familiar with the concept of a "maternal wall."[6] Related to the notion of the glass ceiling, the maternal wall can be seen in the form of bias against women when they are pregnant or become mothers. The number of women who claim they have been discriminated against in the workplace for being pregnant has increased substantially in recent years.[7] Since most women can be seen as potential mothers, there is a significant blurring of the line between gender- and maternal-based discrimination. Even among those women who felt they had put a few cracks in the glass ceiling during the ascent of their careers, many later encountered a maternal wall, prompting them to resign from their jobs. For those who held on to their jobs, many women we interviewed felt they were being blocked from moving upward, or being "mommy tracked," in the institution by some tacit or unwritten set of norms about women, especially married women with children. As one woman said, "I feel like not being available to work late, come in early, and work weekends every weekend has 'mommy tracked' me. It is no longer enough to work nine to five, you have to commit every hour of your life to the job in order to be recognized and get ahead. Those of us trying for balance are perceived as slackers. I was unprepared for this." The ways in which "maternal wall" and "glass ceiling" issues are intertwined can be seen in the comments of a male radiologist, to one of our husbands, who proposed limiting the spots available to women entering radiology residency programs, because, in his practice, the female radiologists, all of whom were mothers, were unwilling to shoulder the same amount of "call" as their male colleagues. In circumstances such as this, all women are subjected to a gender-based "motherhood-by-association" sort of discrimination, even those who intend to remain childless. Therefore, the issues we raise here are relevant to all women, as our research suggests that one's potential to become a mother can act as a tacit job-based barrier.

Another factor pushing women out of the workforce is what sociologist Arlie Hochschild calls the "second shift," meaning the work women do to maintain and sustain the household in addition to their paid employment. The second shift is commonly seen as generating significant stress for American women across the socioeconomic spectrum. National surveys confirm that women take on a disproportionate percentage of housework. For example, the Bureau of Labor Statistics reports that employed, married women with young children do almost two-thirds of the household tasks, with their employed husbands picking up the other third.[8] So while women have made significant gains in the workplace itself, the gender division of labor at home endures. A recent trend to hire household help is opening possibilities to redefine this aspect of women's lives, but even when families hire people to watch their children or clean their homes, women tend to take on the burden of managing the caregivers and any other work that is done in the home. The women we interviewed described trying to balance not only the needs of their children and their jobs, but also their responsibility to manage their homes. For many, the solution was to stay home full-time or to cut back significantly at work.

Therefore, one way to look at all of this is that women quit their jobs or opt off of the "fast track" not for their families but because the pressures and inflexibility of their work situations and their responsibilities for maintaining their families actually leave them no way to maintain both to their satisfaction. This is why many women we spoke with take issue with the term "opting out." Work conditions permitting, many of these women would have preferred to "opt in," albeit on terms that better allowed them both to keep their jobs and to raise their children.

This book provides an overview of the potential deleterious effects of opting out of the labor force for women within and outside of marriage. Yet, we also condition this message with data that documents the steps women can take to minimize economic risk to themselves and to their families. Much of the popular literature on the topic of women "opting out" has had a bit of a doomster tone.[9] While we do not seek to minimize the *potential* for women to be adversely affected by withdrawing from the labor force, we show how women can minimize their risk if this is the option their family uses.

One of the issues we consider is what happens when women give up their paychecks. As one woman aptly noted, "The paycheck gives you a tangible sense of value." Other women we interviewed described how their husband's work time as the sole income earner expands as his home effort decreases dramatically. Still other women lament the loss of what they called their "fuck you money," or the financial independence their own earnings afforded them, which potentially allowed them to leave their marriage if they ever felt they needed to. Still others argue that their "power" within the household did not change because their husbands appreciated the women's efforts at home. The threat that these women might return to work and thus destroy the comfortable support system they provide served to keep these husbands in check.

By leaving work and a paycheck, women who leave their jobs are taking a dramatic step. And, there are risks attached. The average college-educated woman who leaves the workforce today and attempts to reenter later will undoubtedly pay a wage penalty. That said, the risks women take when they reduce or resign their jobs need to be seen within a context that does not rely on a 1950s framework in terms of divorce law and labor force participation of women.

Much has been written about the difficulty of reentering the workforce after significant absences. The limited shelf life of a professional degree presents one significant problem. For example, a physician who does not practice for ten years would have to overcome considerable hurdles to get back into clinical work. On the other hand, opportunities to work in the medical sector of the economy may still be available. Few of the women we interviewed who left their jobs for family reasons sought to return to their original occupations. Some indicated a desire to return to the same field of work, just in a different capacity. Many others said they would prefer to change professions if they returned to work in the future. Some thought of starting their own businesses. Others described transitioning to a caregiving profession. Many of the bond traders, financial managers, and attorneys we interviewed indicated that when, and if, they returned to work they had their eyes on jobs such as elementary school teacher, social worker for the elderly, or patient advocate in hospitals. This observation contributes to how women are seen to leave "fast track" jobs and move into the "second tier."[10] It is impossible to disentangle whether women who leave the labor force change their goals for reentry because they do not feel that it is possible to reenter at the level at which they left, given the status quo, or whether they genuinely seek to reinvent themselves and their career upon returning to paid work after being an at-home mom.

When we look at the landscape for work and families, we do see some evidence that institutions are engaging with the issues we raise here. While we do not see widespread revamping of work in America today—billable hours still reign—there are glimmers of change on the horizon in how some employers are increasing flexible work opportunities for both men and women. Unfortunately, these changes are among the first to be cut under economic constraints.

We argue that more of this kind of change is needed if our society wants to tap into the potential and promise women in the workforce represent. Faced with the current realities of raising children in dual-career families, downsizing or quitting one's job is not only alluring, it is the only way forward for some families. Our research suggests that given the right structure, women who are opting out altogether or who are settling for positions that underutilize their talents could more fully realize their potential to the benefit of themselves, their families, their communities, and the economy. In this respect, the issues these individual women face are not just personal, they are societal. While the concerns of juggling work and family go to the most intimate corners of family life, the implications of women's decisions about paid work concern and affect us all. Recognizing the bedrock reality that these are societal and not personal issues is a critical first step in moving forward to find solutions.

ᴣᴣᴣᴣᴣᴣᴣᴣᴣᴣᴣᴣᴣᴣᴣᴣᴣᴣᴣᴣᴣᴣᴣᴣᴣᴣᴣᴣᴣᴣᴣᴣᴣᴣᴣᴣᴣᴣ

Numbers Too Big to Ignore

Good Work Sister!
We Never Figured You Could Do a Man's Size Job.
WORLD WAR II PROPAGANDA POSTER

ᴣᴣᴣᴣᴣᴣᴣᴣᴣᴣᴣᴣᴣᴣᴣᴣᴣᴣᴣᴣᴣᴣᴣᴣᴣᴣᴣᴣᴣᴣᴣᴣᴣᴣᴣᴣᴣᴣ

The 1970s were heady times for American women, and people often think of the significant presence of women in the U.S. labor force as a phenomenon resulting from the women's movement in the latter half of the twentieth century. On the contrary, women's labor force participation has been on the rise since the late 1800s, and a host of complex and interconnected social and economic factors worked together throughout the twentieth century to move women, and married women in particular, into the paid workforce.[1]

This movement of women into the workforce represents a major demographic shift in American society. Figure 1 illustrates how women's participation in the labor force climbed throughout the 1900s, with a leveling off starting about 1998. This increase stands in stark contrast to men's labor force participation, which stayed roughly stable until it spiked to 88 percent just after World War II, and subsequently dropped steadily to 74 percent by 2008.[2] In contrast, women's participation rose from 18 percent in 1890 to 59 percent in 2008, more than offsetting the declines in male participation.[3]

The only exception to the rise in women's labor force participation occurred just after World War II, when male soldiers returned home and reclaimed their spots in the workforce. Presenting this phenomenon as a steady march into the paid labor force, however, masks interesting variations in the story of women's eco-

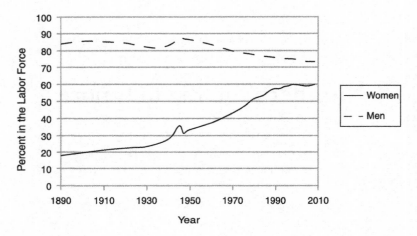

FIGURE 1. Labor force participation rates by gender, 1890–2008

nomic coming-of-age in the last century. While this book focuses on women, families, and work today, it's important to understand how we got here. This understanding allows us to appreciate current conditions and to anticipate directions women's labor force participation may take in the future. In this chapter we briefly trace the twentieth-century evolution of the American economic woman.

Let's be clear at the outset: women have always worked, just not always for pay. In this chapter, we focus on women's movement into the paid labor force, but it's crucial to appreciate that women did not shift from a "nonworking" to a "working" status with this societal transformation.[4] Rather, the change to paid work altered the way that work was recognized and rewarded.

When we say "women," we want to emphasize that employment rates have varied by race and by class. For example, African American women, both single and married, historically have worked at higher rates than white women, and only recently have the participation rates of African American and white women converged, with the difference shrinking to 2.6 percentage points in 2006.[5] If we consider married women, African American women were more than ten times as likely to work as white women in 1890.[6] While still participating at higher rates than white married women,

African American married women in 2006 were only 13 percent more likely to work.[7] And as we will see below, the timing of entry into the labor force depended in large part on socioeconomic class, with working-class and lower-middle-class women entering the labor market before wives in the middle- or upper-income brackets.

The Evolving American Economic Woman

In the agricultural economy, reproductive and productive tasks were closely linked. Women worked alongside men on farms, produced goods such as clothing and soap at home, and were able to care for children while working. Most of women's work was done at home, and young, unmarried women learned skills from their mothers that they themselves employed to run their own households upon marriage.

With the Industrial Revolution, many of the jobs that women, both single and married, had done at home moved to factory-based production. The factory system that evolved during this period increasingly drew a dividing line between production for home and production for the market. While middle-class families were likely to send only men to the paid workforce, working-class families sent men, unmarried women, and children to paid work, reserving home-based production for married women.[8] So at that time, young, unmarried women began to move from producing at home and not for pay, to producing in factories and for pay, thus beginning women's advance into the paid labor force.

In the early part of the twentieth century, most of the women who worked for pay were single. Fewer than 10 percent of married women worked for wages in 1900. Interestingly, when married white women worked for wages, they typically did so only while their children were young, and withdrew as soon as the children were old enough to be employed in the labor force.[9] Indeed, for the first half of the 1900s, marriage marked the end of paid employment for most women. Economist Claudia Goldin writes that "for most of our history, women exited the labor force at the time of marriage, not pregnancy, and their exit was, more often than not, final," and that in the late nineteenth and early twentieth century "marital status, more than any other characteristic save race . . . determined a woman's economic role."[10]

The tide began to turn in the 1920s as married women started to enter the paid labor force in greater numbers. The Great Depression led many married women to seek employment in order to offset the economic strains of income reduction or job loss.[11] During the 1930s, married women's labor force participation grew to about 15 percent. Despite these gains, however, women were increasingly hired into low-status, low-paid, sex-segregated jobs.[12] Newspapers regularly listed help-wanted ads separately for men and women, with the women's jobs usually paying lower salaries. Public acceptance of married women in the workforce was low, however, as social norms at the time dictated that married (white) women should be home with their children, supported by a husband who worked full-time.[13] Many firms and school districts employed so-called marriage bars, policies that barred the hiring of married women and required the firing of single women when they married. These bars remained in place as late as the 1950s in some instances.[14] When the Great Depression waned, many attached a social stigma to the employment of married women, seeing it as an act of economic desperation to be avoided if possible.

When America entered World War II in the 1940s, millions of men left their jobs to become soldiers, and at the same time, the war required a vast buildup of production capacity for military purposes. To ease the resulting massive labor shortage, the U.S. government undertook a major propaganda campaign to encourage all women, and especially married women, to support the military effort by joining the workforce. Thus, Rosie the Riveter was born. One of the most enduring icons of the World War II era, Rosie symbolized the value of women's contributions to the economy and the war effort. Immortalized by posters and even a wartime song of the same name, Rosie helped to recruit women into the paid workforce by appealing to their patriotic duty. Having a wife working in the war effort would not reflect poorly on her husband, nor imply that he could not provide for his family. Rosie helped to reduce the social stigma created when married women sought work during the Great

Depression. Women's paid work, therefore, kept the American economic engine running during this tumultuous period in our nation's history, and their labor force participation during World War II has enduring implications for our economy today.

In response to this call to duty, the female labor force increased by almost 30 percent between 1940 and 1945.[15] Three-quarters of the new female employees were married, and most had school-aged children. Child care centers, financed by the government, sprang up to care for children of mothers working in defense-related industries. At the high point, these centers cared for over 1.5 million children, which interestingly is a higher number than the total of American children in child care in 1974.[16]

When the soldiers returned home, women were laid off or quit their jobs to allow their husbands and brothers to regain employment. Female labor force participation dropped sharply, but never returned to the pre–World War II levels. Many married women remained in the workforce, but found themselves relegated to pink-collar positions, such as clerical or service work. The GI bill paid for returning soldiers to go to college, and as the men availed themselves of this opportunity, their wives then had to work to support the family during that time period. After 1947, women's labor force participation began to climb again, mostly driven by the participation of married mothers, and by 1960, 30 percent of married women worked for pay.

Beginning in the 1960s, however, the pace of entry quickened. The number of women in the workforce increased by 36 percent in the 1960s and by another 44 percent in the 1970s, and increases in married women's participation in the labor force were the engine behind the sharp, overall increases we see for all women during this time.[17] Figure 2 documents this rapid rise of married women's employment, and in particular the employment of married women with children, perhaps the most important demographic labor shift of the twentieth century. Three out of every ten married American women were employed for pay in 1960; by 2005 that rate had more than doubled to over 60 percent.[18] Notably, the entrance of upper-middle-class wives fueled much of the increase in women's

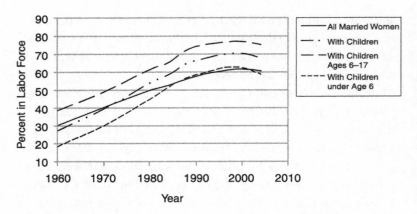

FIGURE 2. Married women's labor force participation by presence and ages of children, 1960–2005

employment in the 1960s and 1970s. The early waves of married women into the workforce were mostly high school graduates, whose family incomes placed them in the lower middle class or working class. The income class of married working women began to change in the 1960s, and Stephanie Coontz reports that the late 1960s marked the first time that college-educated married women were more likely to work than their high school–educated counterparts, and their employment rates have remained higher ever since.[19]

The labor force participation of married women continued to rise through the 1980s and 1990s, although the rate of increase slowed considerably in the 1990s. While the trend of increased participation rates held for all married women, women with older children were more likely than those with infants or preschoolers to work, while those without children were the most likely married women to work.

Forces behind the Evolution

This remarkable movement of married women into the paid workforce often is attributed to the changing social norms associated with the women's movement of the 1960s and 1970s. But as we have seen, a host of complex and interconnected factors worked together to move women, and married women in particular, into the paid workforce. Any increase in employment can be caused by either an increase in the supply of labor, an increase in the demand for labor, or both. In the case of women's entry into the labor force, both factors were at work, and so to help us sort out the complicated forces behind this amazing shift, we categorize the forces into those that propelled women into the workforce and those that increased employer demand for women workers.

From the women's perspective, several factors led to increases in their willingness to work for pay. The nature of work changed, as industry moved from heavy manufacturing toward light manufacturing and the provision of services. These new types of jobs, which were far more likely to be white collar or pink collar, as opposed to blue collar, offered better working conditions and better pay than had been previously available, thus increasing the attractiveness of these positions to women.[20]

Concurrently, the education levels of women increased broadly across the country, and this rise increased women's employment through different channels. Education opened women's minds to possibilities for themselves in the workforce, and also opened up a variety of attractive jobs that had been closed to women in the past. Education also increased women's capacity to earn higher wages, and those increased wages worked to lure more women into the workplace.

At the same time, improvements in household technology made it more feasible for women to complete their household tasks while holding a job outside the home. Refrigeration reduced the need for daily marketing, washing machines and dryers dramatically reduced the labor required for laundry, and processed foods sped up cooking time. However, as we note in chapter 5, while household technology has improved significantly, standards of household production have risen. For example, rising expectations for clean clothing have increased the number of times that laundry must be done per week. As a result, the number of hours spent on household tasks is not as greatly reduced as one would expect. Nevertheless, being able to throw a load of laundry into the clothes washer and then head off to help with a child's homework certainly takes significantly less time than washing with a wringer washer or by hand, line drying, and then assisting with homework.

This is not to underestimate the impact of changing social norms, as they certainly played a tremendous role in the rise in married women's willingness and desire to move into the workforce. Married women's work experience during World War II certainly demonstrated to them and to others that they could handle the jobs. The introduction of the birth control pill and other reliable methods of birth control allowed women to manage, and overall reduce, their fertility. With fewer children at home, married women had greater capacity to divert time to the workforce. Of course, fertility is also likely determined by women's work decisions, as women who are working may opt to have fewer children. Nevertheless, the reduction from four children as the social norm to two children certainly made it easier for women to work for pay outside the home.

On the demand side, many of these same factors prompted employers to want to hire more women. As the nature of work evolved away from heavy manufacturing, which required a certain level of strength, to light manufacturing and services, women's skills became more valuable to employers. While men retained a distinct advantage over women in jobs that required brawn, that advantage waned with the growth of industries, such as services, that required more brain than brawn. Just as women's increased education levels led more married women to supply their labor, those same elevated levels led employers to demand that labor. With higher levels of skills, as evidenced by higher educational attainment, women became increasingly attractive as potential employees.

The overall growth of the economy meant that firms had expanding labor needs. As the economy grew, there just weren't enough men to fill all the positions. During the same period, the post–World War II marriage boom led to a decline in the number of single women available for employment. The demand for women workers exceeded the supply, putting upward pressure on women's wages and also leading to a reduction in legal barriers to married women's employment. Claudia Goldin argues that as women's education levels rose, restricting the pool of workers through the use of marriage bars, for instance, became increasingly expensive.[21] At the same time, changing social norms worked along with the expanded employment needs, and this greater public acceptance of married women in the workforce translated into employers' willingness to hire women.

We would be remiss if we neglected to acknowledge the important role legal changes played in increasing employer demand for women workers. The great social upheaval of the 1960s focused attention on women's rights in the workforce. Title VII of the Civil Rights Act of 1964 codified and helped to solidify those new social norms by making it illegal for employers to discriminate on the basis of race, color, religion, national origin, or sex.[22] That same act created the Equal Employment Opportunity Commission (EEOC) to enforce federal employment discrimination laws.[23] Since that time, the EEOC has doggedly pursued cases of employment discrimination, with each case moving us toward a more equal work environment.[24] While gender discrimination in employment continues today, and we address these issues in chapter 4, the ongoing and public efforts of the EEOC definitely played a major role in increasing employer demand for women workers.

Given these overall upward trends in women's employment, researchers were surprised to see the dramatic rises in women's labor force participation begin to level off starting in the late 1990s, and for some demographic subgroups, such as mothers of infants and mothers with professional degrees, the rates have even declined.[25]

As the labor force participation of married women began to stall, the economy was in the throes of one of the longest peacetime expansions in U.S. history. Then in 2008, America entered into the most serious economic crisis since the Great Depression. As we noted above, in response to the economic hardships of the Depression, women entered the labor force in hopes of at least partially replacing the wages lost by their husbands. In this chapter we trumpeted the rise in women's labor force participation as a sure sign of societal progress, but times of economic crisis led to a flip side we want to acknowledge. The rise of dual-earner couples increased family incomes, but a concomitant rise in consumerism offset the extra income of the second earner. Locked into higher expectations for spending, for many families, it now takes two incomes to meet expenses. Whereas in the past, Dad's income could sustain the family, now it takes both parents' income to do so.[26]

Therefore, unlike in earlier times of economic turmoil, when Dad gets laid off or suffers wage loss, there's no reserve worker at home to send off to look for employment. Mom's already working, and her income is already accounted for in the family budget. And unfortunately, she can be laid off as easily as Dad. So in contrast to the Great Depression, when the number of working women rose, recent recessions have been characterized by declines in women's employment. Whether the economic downturn will have any long-term effects on women's employment in America remains to be seen.[27]

This chapter has focused on the spectacular rise of women in the labor force over the twentieth century. Understanding the factors behind the rise leads us to question the roots of the leveling off and, for some groups, decline in participation rates observed at the millennium. In the following chapter we look more closely at this phenomenon and begin to explore the myriad and complex reasons behind married women's decisions regarding work.

CHAPTER TWO

Why Opting Out Is an Everywoman Issue

My first job in all honesty is going to continue to be mom-in-chief, making sure that in this transition, which will be even more of a transition for the girls . . . that they are settled and that they know they will continue to be the center of our universe.

MICHELLE OBAMA

In 2003, journalist Lisa Belkin wrote a piece for the *New York Times Magazine* called "The Opt-Out Revolution." Belkin interviewed a small group of highly educated women, Princeton alumnae no less, who had "opted out" of the workforce. The reasons women gave for resigning their jobs varied, but all conveyed the sense that when push came to shove, time with their families trumped work. Amply aware of the "hook" potential for this kind of an issue, the media jumped on the bandwagon, spawning a multitude of popular press articles highlighting professional women leaving high-powered jobs. These stories in *Time*, *Business Week*, and *Fortune* sparked a passionate debate on the blogs, at the dinner table, and in book clubs across the country.[1]

This initial media frenzy was followed by a spirited round of rejoinders in the form of books with titles like *Get to Work* and *The Feminine Mistake*.[2] These books warned women of the dangers (to both themselves and to society at large) of recreating a system of dependency on men. In the words of former *New York Times* economics reporter Ann Crittenden describing *The Feminine Mistake*,

"Leslie Bennetts tackles head-on the popular myth that a man is a financial plan."[3] These books seemed to be suggesting that women who left their jobs to raise their children were suffering from some sort of late-onset Cinderella syndrome: when they were younger, they avoided the pitfalls of relying on a Prince Charming character to make all their dreams come true, only to succumb to the promises of a fairy-tale ending once they had a law degree in hand. One characteristic of this "finger wagging" genre of book is that the authors tend to depict women who move out of the labor force as, at best, naïve, and, at worst, dumb; if these women only knew the facts, they would get on the phone to a résumé consultant (as soon as they finished reading the book).

In short, from our own interviews for this project, it seems that many of these accounts underestimated these women who leave the labor force. While we, too, see and point out the very real and potentially deleterious implications of exiting the labor force, we also recognize that the conditions under which twenty-first-century women leave the labor force are different from those of their mothers' and grandmothers' generations.

On the other side of the aisle are authors like Caitlin Flanagan, who is variously characterized as everything from a provacatrice to an antifeminist, and who, in To Hell with All That: Loving and Loathing Our Inner Housewife, trumpeted the movement home. Conservative political activist Phyllis Schlafly, in describing the media attention, said, "[The] feminists are on the run."[4] And this set off another round of fiery responses, further sending the issue into a spiral of polemics.

Beyond the ideological battles being waged over women, motherhood, and feminism, many women found the intense coverage of this issue galling for another reason: nearly three-quarters of married mothers do work, believing their family needs two incomes in order to get by. Why should we care about what could surely be the reality of only an elite few?

In this chapter, we delve deeper into what women who leave their jobs for family can tell us about the struggles of the far broader swath of American women who continue to juggle paid work and family. We argue that instead of treating women who quit their jobs to raise family as peripheral to understanding work in America, we should appreciate the ways in which these women's stories highlight crucial aspects of the realities of combining paid work with raising children. To dismiss women who quit their jobs in the face of competing pressures of work and home as "mythical" is to miss an opportunity to look deeply into the complex and shifting terrain of gender, work, and identity in America.

Squaring Off: Battle of the Numbers

We begin with the numbers, looking at what the experts have to say about the "opt out" phenomenon. Given the generally upward trend in women's labor force participation over the twentieth century, people were surprised to see those numbers begin to stall in the late 1990s. For many women, the signs were first apparent at the places parents hang out with their children—playgrounds and early-childhood education classes. Women standing in the checkout lines in grocery stores were confronted by a phalanx of celebrity moms gracing the covers of magazines—Elle McPherson, Demi Moore, Christie Brinkley. Motherhood had become thoroughly fashionable.

Economic trend spotters, who rely on data generated after the fact, also began to pick up on this phenomenon. The percent of married women who have children under eighteen and participate in the workforce dipped slightly from 73 percent in 2000 to 72 percent in 2003.[5] The largest declines in labor force participation occurred for married mothers of infants, whose participation dropped six percentage points (from 59 percent to 53 percent) between 1997 and 2000, and fluctuated with no clear pattern between 53 and 55 percent through 2007. When we look at college-educated mothers, who have higher than average labor participation rates, the decline is even steeper. The participation rates of these married mothers of infants fell seven percentage points from 71 percent to 63 percent between 1997 and 2005.[6]

As documented in chapter 1, much of the stunning rise in women's labor force participation was driven by the entrance of married mothers during the second half of the twentieth century. In 1975, 47 percent of married women with children under eighteen worked in the labor force. Within the space of a quarter of a century, by 2000, that number had rocketed to a whopping 73 percent.[7] Therefore, to some, while there had certainly been a stagnation in women's participation in the labor force, the declines seemed so small as to be insignificant compared to how far women had come.

Two well-regarded economists have discredited the opt-out argument. Using national labor force participation data, Heather Boushey reported that the stagnation of labor force participation was not limited to married mothers. Married women without children also lowered their participation rates over the same time period. Boushey concluded that the recession of 2001 was the primary force behind any decline in women's participation.[8] Claudia Goldin, who studied women who graduated from elite universities in 1981, found that 58 percent of the women (not all of whom were married) had never been out of the workforce for more than six months. She also found that, at the time of her interview, women with at least one child had spent an average of 2.1 years out of the workforce.[9] Both Boushey and Goldin conclude that the hype surrounding women leaving the workforce is much ado about nothing.

But their research suffers from the limitations inherent in any analysis of labor force statistics. For example, Boushey used labor force participation as her measure of a woman's work. While incredibly useful for understanding the American economy in broad strokes, labor force participation rates mask *intensity* of work. For the purposes of generating a participation rate, a woman is "in" or "out" of the labor force. Boushey, in her analysis, did not consider hours worked or the type of work women were doing. Goldin's analysis was likewise limited by data constraints. Based on an analysis of occupation data for the women in her sample, Goldin concluded that women did not opt out in more subtle ways, such as by choosing less-demanding careers than the ones they were trained for. She found, for instance, that most of the women who had gone to medical school were practicing as doctors by the time they reached their late thirties. But the data she used does not tell us how female medical doctors manage their work hours. For example, in just two years, the percent of women physicians who work part-time rose dramatically, from 8 percent in 2005 to 12 percent in 2007. Both male and female doctors became more likely to work part-time, but the increase was smaller (from 5 percent to 7 percent) for men. Physicians between the ages of thirty-five and thirty-nine are the most likely to work part-time, and in that group, 85 percent are female.[10] To employ a specific example, pediatrics, at 26 percent, leads specialties in the number of part-time physicians. Among graduating pediatric residents, more than half of the females, as compared to 15 percent of their male counterparts, indicated they plan to arrange for a part-time position within five years of completing their residency.[11] These examples provide only one of many illustrations of how "working" versus "not working" fails to capture the complexity of lived experience. While we wouldn't want to extrapolate from the experience of pediatricians to characterize all physicians, nor do we want to assume that the experiences of "all physicians" captures the experiences of female pediatricians.

Therefore, a strength of the type of statistical analysis employed by economists like Boushey and Goldin is that by using large enough samples, economists can move past the experiences of individuals to show trends for populations. But one of the major downsides of using these large samples is that they lack nuance. Limited by the questions the surveyors have asked, economists are often restricted to data sets that already exist. Often, this means viewing trends through the rearview mirror. And when they do their own empirical research, they often rely on quantitative data. In terms of the issue at hand, economists, relying on data collected by the U.S. Census Bureau, track whether people are working or looking for work (that is, "in the labor force") or not working and not looking for work ("out of the labor force"). Finally, another limitation is that economists seldom actually talk to the people they are studying.[12] Therefore, in attempting to understand women's challenges to balance work and family, we must be aware that these statistics mask the myriad trade-offs mothers have made to "make it work."

The Story behind the Numbers

For our analysis, we adopted a mixed methodological approach that combines the kind of big-picture analysis that economists like Boushey and Goldin typically use, with an ethnographic or anthropological approach, or one that privileges the experiences of individual women, as described in their own words. Ultimately, we are interested in charting the forces that shape women's behavior, but of equal importance is how these same women view and make sense of their own behavior. Whereas anthropology has more commonly been associated with studying small, far-flung, "traditional" groups, in this project, we turned the lens on our own society. We analyzed nationally representative data from governmental sources, such as the Current Population Survey of the U.S. Census and the American Time Use Survey of the Bureau of Labor Statistics. Given the limitations of this type of data (as described above), we enriched the statistics with the results of an online anonymous survey of 857 alumnae of a liberal arts college. These women ranged in age from twenty-one to sixty-three and graduated from college between 1970 and 2006. They live in forty-eight states plus the District of Columbia (only Arkansas and Utah are not represented) and thirty-six countries. We conducted 150 formal in-depth and focus group interviews with women from across the country.[13] These interviews were supplemented by another 100 informal interviews with women and men who volunteered their experiences when they learned we were working on this project. We also draw on an anthropological research method called participant observation. We were active participants in many of the settings we include in this book. We have four children between us, ranging in age from three to fifteen. When we are not conducting interviews or teaching or sitting at our computers analyzing data or writing, you'll likely find us volunteering in our child's classroom, carpooling children to baseball games, or working with other parents to organize the school auction or graduation party. While we don't analyze this participant observation material systematically, it informs how we interpret the material gleaned from interviews and the questions we ask of data sets.

Our survey findings, on the surface, tell a story similar to that of what Goldin reports. Over half (57 percent) of respondents had never taken a break from full-time employment of longer than six months, and two-thirds (63 percent) of married mothers with children were working full-time. But in addition to asking these typical labor force survey questions, we also asked more specific questions about their work patterns. Almost half of married mothers (49 percent) indicated that they had at some point in their career reduced their work hours in order to better balance work and family. Over 40 percent had changed jobs for family reasons, and almost one-third had limited work travel for family reasons. Measuring a woman's work simply by whether or not she was employed for pay overlooks the texture of her work experience. Beyond capturing these bright-line differences in terms of sheer numbers, we also sought to capture the areas where the categories of "working" and "not working" blurred.

Therefore, while a two-percentage-point reduction in women's labor force participation rates does not constitute a "revolution," our study findings that describe the many women who otherwise downsize or reorient their careers to better manage family and work are crucial to understanding women's relationship to work. Woman after woman in our study spoke of how she had altered career to accommodate family. They talked about downsizing, reconfiguring, and reimagining their careers. They have reduced travel, turned down promotions, reduced their hours worked, and chosen more flexible (and often lower-paying) work situations. And, in many cases, this process of negotiating a viable solution to accommodate work and family was a struggle.

While the oldest women in our study were pioneers in terms of carving out a new space in the world of work for women, many others we interviewed were likewise pioneering in carving out a space to juggle work and home. Among the women we interviewed, few were able to take advantage of established part-time or other kinds of family accommodation options and had to clear these paths themselves.

The chapters that follow discuss how motherhood shapes women's decisions to resign, reduce, or reorient their careers, and what advantages and disadvantages women see in doing so. We also look at the implications of leaving the workforce. Before we move on to these topics, however, it's important to consider a few additional dimensions of the question of who opts out. Next we provide a set of general characteristics for those who are leaving the labor force or downsizing their careers primarily for family concerns.

The Women behind the Story: Not Just Elites

First, our research shows that, contrary to the sensationalized media reports, women who are downsizing, reorienting, or leaving their jobs entirely are not simply so-called elite women. While the women we studied all have college degrees, their household incomes place most of them in the middle class. Three-quarters of all the women in our survey sample reported household incomes above $50,000. While the majority of the married women in our sample have household incomes below $150,000, 95 percent reported household incomes above $50,000.

Most importantly though, these women are not elites in the sense of those love-to-hate caricatures of women featured in films and books, such as *The Nanny Diaries* and *Momzillas*.[14] While the experiences of women from the Upper East Side of Manhattan have garnered a lot of attention in fictional circles, they are not necessarily representative of the rest of America.[15]

Of the women we interviewed who are now home with their children, many say they feel privileged that their husbands earn enough so they can afford to stay home. But the standard for what is *enough* varies widely across families in the United States. Indeed, the percent of married mothers of infants who stay home full-time increased across all of the income levels between 1997 and 2007, although the increase was steepest among those whose husbands' earnings placed them in the top 20 percent of earners.[16] Trish, one of the mothers we interviewed, challenged the misconception that only wealthy elites become at-home moms:

> I remember when I stayed home with Amy. People would say things like, "It's such a luxury that you get to stay home." But at the time, John and I were making poverty-level income. I remember thinking, "Wait a minute. We're making hardly any money but we're making huge sacrifices to do this." That perception that if you're staying home means you have a lot of money is not true. I remember thinking, "Wait, that's not true!" We're making these choices. We're living in Des Moines, and it was a lot less expensive to live there. It was easier to live on one income there, even though it was almost poverty income [laughing]. But we could do it because our house was $78,000, and you didn't have to drive very far. And so, we could do it.

Still, we realize that the notion of having a so-called choice not to work is available to only a relatively small proportion of American women, while many others need two incomes to keep their household afloat. And in this respect, even though we widen the scope of women who are quitting or cutting back at work to include a broader income group than is commonly perceived, it is still a relatively select group.

AFFORDING NOT TO WORK

When a woman leaves her job to be at home, her family in effect has decided that they can "afford" it, even if the loss of income necessitates financial sacrifices on the part of the household. There are several ways to afford not to work.

The rarest is independent wealth. One at-home mom relayed, "I inherited money from my father . . . so the finances sort of left me free to not have to go the route of a nine-to-five job and day care." Others made enough money to enter into an "early retirement" of sorts. "I have enough assets of my own that I am not dependent upon my husband," one woman told us. "I think it is significant that one spouse could be independently wealthy." However these women came by the assets, independent wealth certainly smoothes the way for some women to leave their jobs. But as we noted above, few of the women we interviewed are independently wealthy.

Another strategy women used to "afford" to quit work was to limit expenses. Employing that age old women's strategy, made famous by singer Peggy Lee, of stretching "a green black dollar bill from here to kingdom come" typifies the tactic many of the women we interviewed who quit their jobs or went part-time used to make up for their lost income. One woman told us, "My husband and I have chosen to live a very modest lifestyle in a very small home, in support of our commitment to my being home." Many couples, such as Trish and her husband, factor in the cost of living in making choices about where to live and how that decision will influence what kind of income the family needs. Therefore, while a part of the story involves families who move from Manhattan to Brooklyn to "make it work," moving from D.C. to Duluth is also a way families make it work. Hence, a wider geographic social field is needed to understand how these processes play out more broadly in America.

Other women, however, indicated that their family was simply able to live on their husband's income, without qualifying that this necessarily entailed sacrifices. Comments such as "my husband makes enough money to support our family;" "I decided not to go back to work because he was making enough money for both of us;" and "I chose to be a stay-at-home parent because I wanted to and we could afford it" are representative of the experiences of some of the women in our sample who are staying home. For many of these women, their ability to stay home is pegged to their husband's success at work. With this observation they suggest that should their husband encounter problems at work, the woman would seek to re-enter the workforce. And this is a matter we revisit in chapter 12.

THOSE WHO'VE LOST THEIR JOBS

Of course, not all women who leave their jobs do so voluntarily. Job displacement represents another shared characteristic of some at-home moms, spanning a wide range of experience from facilitating a graceful and welcome exit to feeling forced out, in part, because of their transition to motherhood. Some women welcomed this displacement because it coincided with their own desire to spend time with their children. A special events coordinator's job was eliminated while she was pregnant. She didn't seek another position and reflected, "If my job had not been eliminated I would have felt compelled to return to it." Less clear on the continuum from voluntary to involuntary displacement were cases of women who gave up their jobs to avoid relocation. One woman called the relocation of her company during her first pregnancy "serendipitous," and admits, "If they hadn't had that little merger and moved . . . I probably would have gone back to work." And, finally, there were women who felt squeezed out of their jobs when they became mothers; this is a topic we will cover in depth in chapter 4.

KINDS OF JOBS

And, finally, job type plays a role in who opts out. We found that certain characteristics, such as the amount of travel required, the frequency of being "on call," and the inflexibility inherent in particular professions, were likely triggers for a woman's decision to drop out of the labor force. We also found that women who have more difficulty going part-time are much more likely to drop out. Unfortunately, a woman's prime childbearing years coincide with the phase of a woman's career that often is the most intense, what Mary Ann Mason and Eve Mason Ekman call the "make or break" years. This combination of high demands, along with the intensity of caring for small children, leads some women to downsize or leave their jobs.[17]

Some women report job dissatisfaction as a reason for leaving their careers, and levels of dissatisfaction seem to vary with the type of career. In a nationally representative survey of highly educated women, only 29 percent of the women who had left their careers for a period of time reported job dissatisfaction as the primary motivator. But if we break that group of women down by field of work, we see a different picture: over half (52 percent) of women with MBAs or other business degrees and almost six out of ten (59 percent) of the female lawyers reported they left their jobs because the work was not enjoyable or satisfying. Doctors and professors seem happier in their work overall, with only 30 percent of medical doctors and 36 percent of academics reporting job dissatisfaction as a major factor in their decision to quit work.[18]

FAMILY FACTORS

While an analysis of data can yield information on the income or job characteristics of mothers who leave as compared to those who stay in the workforce, here, again, the numbers do not tell the full story. Myriad personal reasons may influence a family's decision regarding balancing work and family. Her husband's job demands and how they as a couple negotiate the second shift, or the tasks and time needed to maintain the household; the availability of affordable, high-quality child care; and how the couple approaches parenthood all play important roles in shaping decisions about work and home. We delve into these issues and more in the chapters to come.

Opt-out Dads?

It seems appropriate that we devote some space in this chapter to the men who have left the workforce to care for their children. Men's labor force participation has been dropping steadily since the 1950s, when almost 80 percent of all adult men were employed. In 2005 that number had dropped to 73 percent, and the number is expected to reach 66 percent by 2050. But these numbers are for all men over the age of 16. In our study, we are interested in the work/family decisions families make while they still have children at home. Since most fathers of children under eighteen are between the ages of twenty-five and fifty-five (sometimes referred to as "working-age men"), we are primarily interested in the labor force participation of this demographic. When we look at this group, we see that almost all (91 percent in 2005) working-age men are employed. While the labor force participation of these men has decreased steadily since the mid-1950s when over 97 percent of working-age men were employed, the decreases have been slight, and it remains that over 90 percent of working-age men work for pay in the labor force.[19]

A small, but growing, trend has been in the numbers of dads who stay at home to care for their children. Defining a stay-at-home parent to be one who has been out of the labor force for at least one year for the primary purpose of caring for children, the Census Bureau reports that there were about 159,000 at-home dads in 2006, up from 143,000 in 2005 and 105,000 in 2002. These numbers are dwarfed, however, when compared to the 2.6 million at-home moms in the United States. Only 2.7 percent of full-time, at-home parents are men.[20]

While these numbers are small, they grow larger if we consider men who engage in some type of employment, but still consider themselves to be primary caregivers of their children. For example, almost 20 percent of preschool children are cared for by their fathers while their mothers are at work.[21] Many of these men are employed full-time, just not during the same hours as their wives. These couples primarily work in shifts, so as to limit the hours their children spend in nonfamily care. Another growing subgroup, however, includes men who, while they work in some type of part-time employment, consider themselves to be "at-home" dads.

We talked with men who wanted to help their wives flourish in their careers by putting their own careers on hold. While a few men were fully unemployed, most at least dabbled with some type of paid employment. One stepfather of two boys explained that his second wife was younger than he, and at a stage where her career could really take off. He had enjoyed a successful business career and was willing to stay home with their sons so she could go full throttle at work. But he wouldn't have been classified by the Census Bureau as a "stay-at-home" dad. He bought a shop and hired employees to staff it during the week. He worked in the store on weekends while his wife was home. Another father of three, whose wife is the CEO of a medium-sized human resources company, manages a "small hedge fund of sorts" while taking care of his children. One edits the neighborhood paper. Another is an artist. Another is a rare-book collector. Another sells automotive parts on Ebay.

Regardless of whether they are "full-time," these stay-at-home dads provide the backbone for the careers of many successful women. Sally, who works at the director level for a major phar-maceutical company, told us that she is thinking of trying to "get a stay-at-home husband" because all of the women at the executive director level had one: "If you don't have a stay-at-home husband, you don't get to be on the executive committee." In another case, the CEO of a health care organization gestured toward the other women at a women's economic leadership roundtable, and said that almost all of them (including herself) have husbands at home managing their family lives. These couples go against the traditional model of having Mom stay home while Dad goes to work. But in some ways, it's just the gender that's changed, not the constraints that led them to decide that one parent would stay home.

So although Lisa Belkin described the experiences of a few elite women, it is clear that women across an income spectrum face similar trade-offs between work and family. While the sheer number of women who have "opted out" may not constitute a revolution, their experiences allow us greater insight into the lives of working mothers generally. In the chapters to come, we delve more deeply into the experiences of mothers who have chosen to opt out from or downsize their careers, and from that gain a deeper understanding of women, work, and identity in America.

‿‿‿‿‿‿‿‿‿‿‿‿‿‿‿‿‿‿‿‿‿‿‿‿‿‿‿‿‿‿‿‿‿‿‿‿‿‿

CHAPTER THREE

The 100-Hour Couple

The hurrieder I go, the behinder I get.

OLD PENNSYLVANIA DUTCH ADAGE

‿‿‿‿‿‿‿‿‿‿‿‿‿‿‿‿‿‿‿‿‿‿‿‿‿‿‿‿‿‿‿‿‿‿‿‿‿‿

One of the most intriguing explanations for why women leave the workforce or reorient their careers is the phenomenon of the 100-hour couple. Valerie's story gives us some insight into how these tough decisions play out among high-achieving couples. Valerie was an English and political science double major in college. A child of a widowed mother who single-handedly supported and raised five children, Valerie attended a state university and worked her way through college. She went on to attend law school and to work as a corporate attorney. Eventually, she married an attorney, Richard, who worked in banking. By the time they had their second child, their careers were at a zenith, with Valerie and her husband each working an average of seventy hours per week. To cover the seventy hours of child care, they hired a full-time, live-in nanny and a part-time nanny. When they discovered they needed yet a third nanny because work obligations increasingly spilled into evenings and weekends, they decided to reevaluate their situation. They concluded that one of them had to reduce hours at work or quit his or her job altogether. They recognized that they could live on either Valerie's or Richard's salary alone, although his income was significantly larger than hers. Therefore, for financial as well as for other less tangible reasons that could not be tallied on a spreadsheet, Valerie decided to leave her job and to stay home with their children.

Valerie's case illustrates some key points. Over the past decades, women's educational qualifications have risen. Similarly, their job aspirations have expanded outward and upward. These well-educated women now compete for high-powered, high-paying jobs. Many marry spouses who have followed a similar educational and professional trajectory. Concurrently, work-time demands for these high-paying jobs have increased dramatically. So what we are seeing with this shift in women's educational and career achievements is a transition to the high-powered couple, resulting in a rapid and significant increase in the percent of high-earning couples who together work extremely long hours, over one hundred hours per week. We call these families "100-hour couples."

Valerie and her husband were on the upper end of the hours scale, clocking in over 140 hours per week, but still their struggles and decision making mirror those of couples who find themselves trying to manage their families with each working 50 or more hours per week.[1] In this chapter we explore in depth the factors that contribute to the development of the 100-hour couple: increases in women's education and job aspirations, along with significant increases in the time demanded in certain types of jobs.

Increases in Women's Educational Achievements

The 100-hour couple has its origins in the great strides made in women's education over the past generation. The educational aspirations of women in the twentieth century moved from the desire to graduate from eighth grade to an expectation for high school graduation, and perhaps even college. In 1940, 60 percent of American women had completed fewer than nine years of schooling. By 1957, over 64 percent of women had at least a high school degree, but only 7 percent had graduated from college.

The women's movement of the 1970s heralded a striking rise in women's college-education rates. While in 1970 only 8 percent of American women held college degrees, that number had more than tripled by 2007, when 26 percent of American women held college degrees. Although men overall are still more likely to have a college degree than women, young women now have the advantage over their male counterparts, with 34 percent of twenty-five- to thirty-four-year-old women holding a college degree as compared to 28 percent of similarly aged men.[2] If these trends continue, we can expect that American women will soon be more educated than American men.

In tandem with increases in the number of women earning college degrees, the number of women with graduate and professional degrees has also grown. Roughly half of all entering students in medical and law schools are now female. Other formerly male educational bastions such as veterinary school are now more than 80 percent female. The number of women enrolled in business schools still lags behind other professional programs, but even here women now constitute about one-third of enrollments, a significant increase over the past twenty-five years.[3]

Higher Education Leads to Higher-Profile Jobs

As women have met, and in some cases even surpassed, the education levels of their male counterparts, they have made steady inroads into jobs that were formerly held almost exclusively by men. Women's increased education has opened doors to high-profile positions. According to the U.S. Census Bureau, in 2000, women made up just over one-half of professional and managerial workers.[4]

Higher female enrollment in medical schools has led to substantial increases in the number of female medical doctors. In 1970, only 8 percent of physicians were women, and while the concentration varies by specialty, in 2006 that percentage had risen to 28 percent.[5] While women comprise 44 percent of obstetricians and gynecologists, pediatrics is the only subspecialty in which women actually outnumber men.[6]

In another traditionally male domain, women now enter the legal profession at rates comparable to men, but they are more likely than men to accept certain kinds of positions, such as judicial clerkships, government positions, or public-interest jobs. Women have also moved into the judiciary. In 2007, 25 percent of circuit court judges were women, and nineteen state courts of last resort, sometimes referred to as supreme courts, had a female chief justice. Women have moved into high-ranking legal positions in corporations as well; 16 percent of the Fortune 1,000 General Counsels are female.[7] Women are less likely than men to enter private practice.[8] Still, perhaps in direct relationship to their numbers in law schools, women comprise 44 percent of associates in private law firms. As women move up the ranks, their attrition rate is substantially higher than that of men. Only 16 percent of partners in those same law firms are women. While law firms have long argued that these numbers are caused by a "pipeline issue," meaning it will take time for the older, male-dominated cohorts of partners to retire, the high numbers of women law students since the 1980s should have by now made it through that pipeline. Indeed, among lawyers who graduated in the past fifteen to twenty-five years, where most of the graduating classes were between 40 and 50 percent female, women make up only 20 percent of partners.[9] For reasons that we discuss later, it is particularly challenging for a woman to be a partner at a major law firm.

Nonetheless, it is clear that women have parlayed their educations into higher-profile positions in the labor force, and these jobs pay well. The average compensation in the United States is $213,000 for a lawyer and $316,000 for an obstetrician/gynecologist.[10] While the pay is quite good, these jobs also require a substantial time commitment. Corporate executives, lawyers, and physicians routinely work fifty-plus hours per week, and physicians compound these hours with overnight shifts.

Lawyers in Love

Most college-educated married people meet their spouse either at school or on the job. In our survey sample, for example, 43 percent indicated they met their spouse either in college or graduate school, with an additional 18 percent who met their spouse at work. A 2006 Harris Interactive study of 2,985 adults (not all college educated) found that 32 percent of those married or in a relationship met their partners in school or at work.[11] Given the rise in women's educational achievements, along with their increased presence in managerial and professional jobs, well-educated women gravitate toward high-powered, high-paying jobs. Since couples often meet at school or work, it follows that these trends have led to couples in which both partners are qualified for and pursue demanding, high-stress jobs.

There are many theories to explain how individuals find each other as marriage partners. If you believe opposites attract, then you might subscribe to the negative assortative mating theory. The basic argument for negative assortative mating goes like this: men and women choose mates who will complement their skills. So a man who is highly productive in the workforce will choose a partner who has the skills to manage the domestic part of his life. In this case, the husband would work in the labor force and the wife in the home. Thus, each partner would work exclusively, or specialize in, their area of expertise (economists call this working to one's comparative advantage) and reap the greatest economic returns.[12] This model works well in predicting the traditional gender-based division of labor in the 1950s, where Dad went to his job and Mom managed the home.[13]

Positive assortative mating, on the other hand, means choosing to marry someone who is like you. This theory, which perhaps holds more sway today, argues that people who share similar interests, educations, and cultural values are more likely to marry (and to stay married). These couples are more likely to enjoy spending leisure time together engaged in similar pursuits and thus have higher levels of satisfaction in their marriages. Studies show that since the 1960s, couples are increasingly likely to have similar education levels, especially among college graduates. Interestingly, data also show that pairing by education level actually declined between 1940 and 1960.[14] This decline may have been, in part, related to the fact that men increased their education levels before women did. Other studies examine how a woman's status in the labor market affects her marriage prospects. For example, a 2004 study noted that women's wages before marriage are highly correlated with her husband's occupation and future earnings potential, and that relationship has been strengthening over time.[15] In other words, the more money a single woman earns, the more likely she now will be to marry a man with potential for high earnings and occupational status.

The women we interviewed enjoyed their work and, for the most part, did not begrudge the time required to get their jobs done. But sometimes problems surfaced when their families, or even their desire to have a family, were compromised by the resulting stresses of the considerable time requirements of their job. For some, as illustrated by one of the women we surveyed, the grueling hours at work made meeting a spouse even more difficult: "I took a break for one plus years *because* (emphasis hers) I was working so hard that I didn't have time for a spouse, partner, or children." For others, fertility problems led to a rethinking of work priorities. Another woman we surveyed said, "I worked every day after graduating from college but never considered not working until my fourth miscarriage, at which time I sought to reduce my 'work' hours." For many others, though, the arrival of children triggered their decision to reduce their work hours. We address these complicated issues in later chapters.

Meet the 100-Hour Couple

In the early 1990s, Juliet Schor's book *The Overworked American* argued that Americans were working longer hours than they had in previous decades, at the expense of leisure. Specifically, she estimated that while annual paid work hours rose for both men and women between the late 1960s and the late 1980s, women's annual hours rose substantially more (by 305 hours) than did men's (by 98 hours).[16]

Striking a chord with the American public, Schor tapped into a deeply held feeling that families, and women in particular, felt overwhelmed by their work and family responsibilities, in ways that their parents and grandparents had not. The appearance of *The Overworked American* on the *New York Times* best-seller list for multiple weeks demonstrates how powerfully her arguments spoke to the American public.

Despite the resonance of her argument and the popularity of her book, Schor's findings are suspect. While annual hours worked did rise during that time period, the average hours worked per week did not actually change very much. In fact, the length of the average workweek remained fairly constant between 1970 and 1997. What did rise substantially was *number of weeks worked*, as more women entered the workforce.[17] Therefore, the increase in annual hours worked resulted from increases in the number of weeks worked per year, in particular by women. Of course, women's labor force participation climbed steadily during that period. If a woman started a job in October of 1980 and worked continuously through December of 1981, she would be counted as working twelve weeks in 1980, but fifty-two weeks in 1981. The data would show that there was an increase in weeks worked (and thus total hours worked) between 1980 and 1981, but that increase was caused by a rise in labor force participation, not by a change in the hours per week demanded by employers.

So if average weekly work hours have not increased, how is it that so many women we interviewed felt so increasingly pressed for time? The answer lies in a more nuanced look at the data. Weekly hours for most segments of the population have stagnated or fallen, but at the same time, at the high end of the income distribution the fraction of people who work extremely long hours has increased substantially.[18] And as we documented earlier, these same people are also more likely to be married to other "overworked" Americans. This is where the 100-hour couple notion becomes important.

As women entered the labor force, families began to abandon the male breadwinner model, and dual-career couples became more commonplace. In 1970, just over one-third of married couples were both earning an income. By 2000, that number had jumped to almost 60 percent.[19] So even though the average hours worked by an individual may not have changed, married couples may have felt an increase in hours labored during their shared workweek.

As the number of dual-career families increased, another phenomenon was under way. The fraction of men who work long hours (defined as fifty or more hours per week) began to rise in 1970. These shifts were most dramatic for high-earning and college-educated men, men at the top of the income ladder who are more likely to earn a salary as opposed to an hourly wage. For example, between 1979 and 2002, the fraction of college-educated men who worked long hours rose by 37 percent.

Historically, lower-income men have worked the longest hours, but in the final two decades of the twentieth century, that trend began to reverse. In 1983, the lowest-paid 20 percent of employed men were more likely to work long hours than the highest-paid 20 percent. But by 2002, the high-income earners were more than twice as likely to work long hours as were the lowest-paid 20 percent. In fact, long workweeks rose by 80 percent among earners in the top 20 percent of the income ladder.[20]

These extremely long work hours certainly reduce the time available for family. Sociologists Jerry Jacobs and Kathleen Gerson report that almost half of people who work fifty or more hours per week regularly work during weekends, and most of them report devoting one weekend day to work. (Just over half of men who work fifty-plus hours per week indicate that they regularly work on the weekend, as compared to 42 percent of women.) While these 100-hour couples certainly do not represent the average dual-earner couple (who in 2000 jointly worked eighty-two hours per week), Jacobs and Gerson report striking increases in the percent of couples who work one hundred or more joint hours, rising from 8.7 percent of married couples in 1970 to 14.5 percent in 2000.[21]

Long work hours seem to be concentrated in managerial, professional, and technical occupations. One in three men who work in such positions report working long hours, as compared to one in five men in other occupations. For women, the difference is even more striking, with one in six of those in professional and managerial positions reporting long workweeks, as compared to one in fourteen in other occupations.[22]

The reasons for these dramatic increases are varied. Economists Peter Kuhn and Fernando Lozano explain this phenomenon using the concept of what they call a "long hours premium," in other words, the increased salary generated by working extra hours. If the long hours premium rose over time, then the incentives to working longer hours would have increased. Kuhn and Lozano find that the long hours premium did rise, and that these increased incentives led men to increase their work hours. For example, in the early 1980s, a salaried man who worked fifty-five hours per week could expect to earn about 10 percent more than one who worked forty hours per week. That gap more than doubled to 25 percent by 2002.[23] Even though salaried workers do not receive "overtime pay," per se, they can expect to reap rewards of the extra hours over the long run, perhaps in the form of a bonus or a promotion. While this study applied to men, it is reasonable to assume that the long hours premium, while perhaps smaller, would also exist for women.

Some attribute the push among high-income workers to work even longer hours to a "keeping up with the Joneses" mentality. Studies have shown that happiness depends not just on absolute income, but perhaps even more so on relative income. This line of research indicates that if you make $100,000 per year, but you live and work among people who earn $300,000 per year, you will not be as happy as you would if you lived and worked with people who earned $70,000 per year.[24] This drive to earn more relative to a comparison group can lead people to work ever-increasing numbers of hours. A prime example can be found in the attitudes of the "working-class millionaires" of Silicon Valley. A 2007 *New York Times* article described couples whose net worth put them in the top 1 percent of the richest families in the United States, yet who still felt their incomes to be lacking. Comparing themselves to those with more, many of these people worked sixty to seventy hours per week because they felt that what they had wasn't enough.[25]

Of course, increased work hours may also come at the requirement of the employer. As we detail in chapter 4, employers have increased expectations for the work hours and availability of employees, especially in the managerial and professional ranks. Technological advances such as the Blackberry, iPhone, and high-speed Internet access enable twenty-four-hour accessibility to employers and clients. Globalization has increased requirements for travel abroad.

Thus, with this larger pool of well-educated, well-employed women, we have transitioned to high-powered couples, resulting in a rapid and significant increase in the percent of high-earning couples that together work over one hundred hours per week. The combination of the high stress associated with killer hours and the income stream to afford living in a single-earner household provides a set of conditions in which many highly educated women ultimately reduce their work hours or drop out of the workforce completely.

And this brings us back to Valerie and Richard, the 100-hour couple we introduced at the outset of this chapter. In Valerie's life we see many of the themes we've discussed here. Her hard work in conjunction with an expanded range of educational options for women resulted in her ability to achieve educationally and professionally what would have been very difficult to do a generation earlier. Meeting and marrying Richard, her educational and professional equal, is what we would expect, if the theory of positive assortative mating holds true.

Yet, when Valerie and Richard did "everything right" by jumping through all of the societal hoops put before them, they found that their jobs drained them not only of their time but also of their energy. Their children were being raised by staff, and they rarely had time to relax and enjoy the kids. To make their lives work, everything had to be very highly scheduled. The stress led them, like so many other couples in their position, to decide that Valerie would shelve these hard-earned educational achievements, at least for the time being, and quit her job.

In later chapters, we revisit Valerie and Richard's decision for her to leave the workforce instead of Richard leaving or, alternatively, both of them cutting back at work. How this particular family managed the stresses of the 100-hour couple is reflective of broader societal themes surrounding gender and work in America.

CHAPTER FOUR

Glass Ceilings
and Maternal Walls

*Pick young married women. They usually have
more of a sense of responsibility than their
unmarried sisters, they're less likely to be flirtatious,
they need the work or they wouldn't be doing
it, they still have the pep and interest to work
hard and to deal with the public efficiently.*
"GUIDE TO HIRING WOMEN," 1943

When young women graduate from college today, they expect that they will enter into the labor market on the same terms as men. They expect to be able to hold the same jobs as men, and to earn similar salaries as well. And, in some niches of the labor market, this expectation is realized. Without children, men and women pursue their careers neck in neck in terms of pay when they work similar jobs for similar hours. In fact, the gender wage gap for childless people between the ages of twenty-seven and thirty-three is practically zero. Unfortunately, however, while this parity gives us a glimpse of what is possible, it does not reflect widespread reality. In fact, women experience the labor market differently from men, in both explicit and tacit ways, and these differences in experiences have dramatic effects on women's economic position. Women earn less than men, on average, and they are far less likely to hold leadership positions.[1] And, as we show throughout this book, women are far more likely than men to reduce their work commitments in order to manage their families.

This chapter explores the ways in which gender discrimination shapes women's experiences on the job. In so doing, it illustrates the decline of overt discrimination alongside the simultaneous persistence of more subtle, even tacit, forms of gender-based discrimination. Appreciating the enduring relevance of gender-based discrimination at work is important to understanding the overall context in which women make decisions about combining career and family.

Two ways of thinking about gender-based discrimination at work are glass ceilings and maternal walls. Popularized by the *Wall Street Journal* in the mid-1980s, the term "glass ceiling" refers to subtle barriers that impede the career advancement of women and minorities. The ceiling is glass because while the path to promotion seems clear, these invisible barriers prevent women from reaching the top levels in their careers. By the mid-1990s, people were also reckoning with what came to be called the "maternal wall," where parents, and predominantly mothers, are the victims of workplace bias on the basis of having family responsibilities.[2] These two forms of barriers featured prominently in our interviews with women who had decided to leave or downsize their careers. In the sections that follow, we juxtapose women's gains at the workplace over the past century with the enduring dilemmas they face today.

Discrimination

Let's consider first the issue of discrimination. Discrimination against women at work takes many forms, and may be perpetrated by employers, co-workers, or customers. Specifically, discrimination occurs when two equally qualified people are treated differently solely on the basis of membership in a particular group, such as gender or race. When employers make hiring, promotion, or salary decisions purely based on someone's gender, they are discriminating. As we discussed in chapter 1, the Civil Rights Act of 1964 made it illegal for employers to discriminate on the basis of sex. This legislation, along with the factors that made women more attractive workers to employers, led to a significantly more equal workplace.

Employers no longer can discriminate overtly against women with impunity.

Changes in the legal system and social norms have led to a far more equal workplace. Nevertheless, despite the great strides made in the past forty years, discrimination on the basis of gender continues in the workforce. A recent snapshot of all discrimination suits filed with the Equal Employment Opportunity Commission in 2007 shows that charges filed on the basis of gender (30 percent) approached that of the number filed on the basis of race (37 percent).[3]

Specific illustrations of gender discrimination abound. One well-publicized case was that of the "Boom-Boom Room." In this case, Wall Street's unacceptable behavior toward women was exposed in the mid-1990s when current and former Smith Barney employees filed a class action sexual harassment and discrimination suit. The suit "outed" Smith Barney's Boom-Boom Room, a basement party room in a Long Island office where the male brokers created an *Animal House* atmosphere. That suit opened the floodgates, and a series of suits against other major brokerage houses ensued. These women brokers asserted that they had been intimidated, subjected to X-rated jokes, and excluded from business lunches, and that their careers were damaged as a result of this inappropriate behavior. These gross misbehaviors, along with discriminatory compensation packages, were the basis of the lawsuits that rocked the financial district and led to significant payments to the women affected.[4]

While many argue that gender-based discriminatory practices are a thing of the past, women continue to file and win discrimination suits. Yet another sex discrimination class action suit was filed against Smith Barney in 2005.[5] American Express settled a discrimination suit for $31 million in 2002, and implemented a series of reforms, including changing the way new accounts were distributed among employees.[6] And, of course, these suits are not limited to the financial world. The United States Air Force settled a gender discrimination suit in 2008, filed by civilian Suzanne A. Mertes, who claimed that management refused to promote her into a supervisory position, despite her qualifications, on the basis of her gender. Mertes claimed she was called a bitch, a troublemaker, and a complainer. The Air Force agreed to pay $490,000 plus back pay and also promote her to a supervisory position.[7]

For many younger women, especially, descriptions of cases like the Boom-Boom Room seem almost to belong to another era, even though the events described occurred not that long ago. What this signals, perhaps, is that thanks in part to the legal system, society is far less tolerant of such egregious acts of discrimination. While as we have seen, some employers continue to openly discriminate, most employers understand the legal ramifications of overt discrimination, and this understanding has led to shifts in the way women are treated at work. As a result, discrimination on the basis of gender today is far more likely to be subtle than overt. Few of the women we interviewed indicated they had been subjected to sexual harassment or other outright discriminatory acts. They were far more likely to mention the more subtle ways that their gender or maternal status presented obstacles in the workplace.[8] In the sections below we explore some of these more subtle ways gender continues to shape women's experiences at work.

Glass Ceilings

In contrast with these stories of overt discrimination, many of the women we interviewed, in fact, reported excelling on the job in their years before having children, competing with men point for point, client for client, case for case. And, it is critical to appreciate that even though we are focusing on some of the impediments women face at work, some women are phenomenally successful at what they do. One now at-home mother noted, "I was pretty successful. Analysts were kind of like rock stars of the finance world." Many of the women reported that they loved their jobs—the adrenaline rush, the competition, the excitement.

The fact that some of the women we interviewed excelled in their careers does not mean that they did not encounter what is commonly called the glass ceiling; it just means that they developed strategies to maneuver through a series of obstacles to rise nearer to the top. Some of the maneuvers women described were adapting to male culture at work and making inroads into the "old boys' network."

A glass ceiling that women we interviewed felt they had learned, for the most part, to work around was that of the male-dominated work culture. One way women executives do this is developing styles that put men at ease. Valentina, a Stanford Business School graduate, described her initiation to her job as one of four women out of one hundred revenue producers at an investment bank. Within the first week, each of the other three female analysts took her aside and shared tips for how to negotiate the male work culture. One particularly memorable lesson had to do with managing one's emotions. Crying, as a manifestation of stress or fatigue, one of them relayed, "was not good and made their male colleagues very uncomfortable." At home that night, her husband advised that if she ever felt herself on the brink of tears, she should, instead, "take her hand and wham it on the table, and say 'Goddammit, I'm not putting up with this,' and leave, which none of the men has a problem with. And then you go off and put yourself back together in the restroom and lay low until you've got yourself back under control. It works like a charm." Valentina employed this strategy from time to time and found that her male colleagues were completely comfortable with this type of behavior. Given the small number of women in these top positions, Valentina was lucky to have women mentors (and a husband) who taught her this cultural rule. Yet, at the same time, this example is troubling because it illustrates the extent to which women have to adapt to male cultural norms at work, rather than the workplace transforming to accommodate women. We will revisit this topic when we discuss the intersection of work expectations and caregiving responsibilities.

Valentina's experience is far from atypical. Linguist Deborah Tannen, in her classic book *Talking from 9 to 5*, documented systematically how conversational-style differences at work serve as a glass ceiling for women (and others who were historically not "typical" employees).[9] Echoing one of Tannen's examples, a female college professor we interviewed described how she still, well into her career, had to check herself *not* to respond with "I don't know; I'll find out for you," when a student asked her a question in class that she couldn't answer. Following the lead of male colleagues, she schooled herself to place the burden for finding out back on the student or otherwise creatively dodge the question until the next class when she could address it more knowledgeably. Other women spoke of learning to "take your lumps," and to "never say you're sorry."

Overall, many of the women we interviewed explained how they had learned the cultural rules for how to talk and how to behave in these male-dominated settings. And, it appears that women have had more success in breaking through the glass ceiling of male culture in some fields than in others. The Center for Work-Life Policy, a nonprofit organization that studies women and work, recently reported that women in science, engineering, and technology fields are likely to leave their positions, in large part "because the hostility of the workplace culture drives them out. If machismo is on the run in the United States, then this [science, engineering, and technology fields] is its Alamo—a last holdout of redoubled intensity."[10] With over half of the women in the industry leaving between the ages of thirty-five and forty, the attrition rate is double that for men and is significantly higher than for women in law or finance. Therefore, while learning male cultural rules is a way for some women to break through, it is not a multipurpose solution.

Women encountered other glass ceilings in recruiting practices that use the "old boys' network" or business conducted on the golf course or in the locker room after a game of squash. In a 2003 study of female corporate executives, 41 percent listed exclusion from informal networks as a top barrier to their career advancement.[11] Many women executives report taking up golf and peppering their conversations with sports analogies as ways to break down these barriers.[12] It's a bit trickier for these women to figure out how to get into the men's locker room. One woman we interviewed described a scene that illustrates this point piquantly. Immediately following a presentation she had made to a group of senior executive vice presidents of a large international corporation, the group took a break. The male executives ambled toward the men's room. The sole female executive followed closely, stuck her foot in the door before it closed, and shouted, "Now don't go making any decisions in there without me." In another case, a professor described the situation at the college where she worked: When she and other female faculty members learned that their new provost would be a woman, several commented, "We'll finally have equal access to our boss." The previous provost was known for running each day at noon, and many male faculty members took advantage of the locker room as a predictable opportunity for communicating with him. The new provost wasn't a runner, and locker-room access didn't emerge as a gendered point of access for women in the same way as it had for men with the male provost, but many felt that having neither males nor females with locker-room access to the provost leveled the playing field for all.

So, while there are ways women can make inroads into the old boys' network, it remains a glass ceiling for many. And, as we will describe below, finding time to participate in out-of-work social bonding and networking events, such as happy hour after work or golf on weekends, becomes increasingly difficult when the competing demands of family caregiving are factored in.

Among the obstacles to women's success in the workplace, a particularly hard-to-beat barrier lies in the stereotyping of women's capabilities. Unlike learning to talk like a man at work or honing your golf skills, being the victim of stereotyping can be trickier because the situation does not just rely on what you do, but also on others' perceptions of you. These perceptions can be a reaction to you as an individual, but they can also be a reaction to the stereotypes of "people like you"—in this case, women.

Catalyst, a leading research and advocacy organization for corporate women, reports that one-third of female corporate executives found stereotyping and preconceptions of women's roles and abilities to be a significant barrier in their careers.[13] Stereotyping may lead men to exclude women from informal networking and mentoring, which in turn may limit women's access to assignments and promotions. A 2007 study concluded that "gender stereotypes lead organizations to routinely underestimate and underutilize women's leadership talent."[14] The same study concluded that while men are considered to be default leaders, women leaders are considered to be atypical or violating accepted norms of leadership. In effect, this places women in a "damned if you do and damned if you don't" situation. If they lead in a manner consistent with gender stereotypes, they are seen as too soft, and not as leaders. At the same time, if they go against the stereotype, they are considered overly aggressive—competent, but not particularly well liked.

Maternal Walls

No matter what a woman's plans or goals regarding reproduction are, stereotyping women's capabilities seems inextricably bound up in actual or potential motherhood. The number of women who claim they have been discriminated against in the workplace for being pregnant has increased substantially in recent years.[15] And there is no bright-line distinction between discrimination on the basis of gender and discrimination on the basis of one's actual or potential status as a mother.

Even among those women who felt they had put a few cracks in the glass ceiling during the ascent of their careers, many later encountered a maternal wall, prompting them to resign from their jobs. For those who held on to their jobs, many women we interviewed felt they were being blocked from moving upward, or being "mommy tracked," in the institution by some tacit or unwritten set of norms about women, especially married women with children. One of the women we surveyed told us, "When I had my first child everyone expected that I would reduce my interest and activity level at work. I was sometimes not invited to meetings as people thought I would not like to add 'extra' elements to my work. There are plenty of working moms who hit it hard [pursue their work vigorously]." Another woman noted, "I took only ten weeks with the birth of each child, working until my due date. After the birth of the second child, I changed positions sufficient to reduce travel, but not total work effort. However, the fact of children created the (unstated) belief by my employer of lack of 'true' commitment; hence, the glass ceiling."

These women, like so many others who work full throttle at their jobs, did not want to reduce their responsibilities at work. The workplace is full of highly committed mothers who work just as hard as they did before they had children. Some mothers feel that their employers created environments in which they could successfully combine full-tilt employment with raising children. These women often relied heavily on dependable child care. One woman who worked for a large international corporation reflected on how her employer made a difference for her: "The good thing about working for [her employer] is that they were so conscious of being equal opportunity employers. They really did extend themselves to women, and that included [accommodating women] having children." At the same time, though, she also credited a large part of her professional success to having a live-in nanny, allowing her to focus on her career.

Unfortunately, in many cases, maternal status does lead employers to treat women differently. In one eye-opening case, Sandra, a regional vice president for a furniture manufacturer in Philadelphia, took six weeks off with her first child, putting her son into family day care from 7 a.m. to 7 p.m. when she returned to work. Later, around the time when her second child was born, her company was bought out by a larger firm, which meant merging three smaller companies. For Sandra, this meant an opportunity for advancement in her career, as she was now responsible for a larger region and sales organization. At the conclusion of the merger, however, there were a number of displaced vice presidents, and one in particular who wanted to move back to Philadelphia. One day, her bosses came to her home: "I was still nursing. They came to my house when I was four weeks postpartum. They came in a limo while I was nursing on the couch. They said, 'Oh Sandra, you just had a baby, you should move back into sales.' And they gave [this VP] my job. They said they'd keep me at the manager salary level. 'You can work from home one day a week. Just let him have this job. Don't put up a fight.' I took the offer. I had to have a job to go back to.

When I left I was a regional manager and when I went back I was a sales rep, and I only took six weeks off. I didn't have much choice other than leave the company. I'd had eleven years' tenure there."

And, of course, Sandra's case is not isolated. In 2007, women who claimed they were demoted or had their pay cut after becoming pregnant and taking maternity leave filed a class action lawsuit against Bloomberg L.P., the financial-services and media company founded by New York City mayor Michael Bloomberg.[16] This suit argued that motherhood, as opposed to gender, was the primary trigger of the discrimination. The Pregnancy Discrimination Act of 1979 prohibits discrimination on the basis of pregnancy, childbirth, and related medical conditions.[17] A consequence of this law is that firms must treat pregnancy leave as they would any other disability leave, and this is particularly important when calculating retirement benefits, because it means that women should receive seniority credit while on maternity leave. In 2008, the U.S. Supreme Court heard arguments on whether AT&T is discriminating by paying smaller retirement checks to women who took leave before the law was passed, effectively reducing their seniority credits for the time they were on leave.[18] Therefore, while in many ways our society seems to have moved beyond the Boom-Boom Room, in other, more subtle ways, we have not. The question then is: what would it take to move beyond discrimination to create a more equitable work environment for women, and for anyone who seeks to combine paid work with caregiving responsibilities?

The Ideal Worker

A reverberating theme in our interviews was the reality that in many instances jobs were structured to meet the capabilities of married men with a stereotypical wife at home willing to manage their home lives. And, as argued in chapter 3, this is a problematic scenario for families when the wife is also in the boardroom or the operating room.

As legal scholar Joan Williams has argued, the American ideal worker norm leads employers to expect complete dedication from their employees, a commitment that takes precedence over any other commitments.[19] Some employers expect their employees to be available for meetings, regardless of the hour. Others require extensive travel, or even relocation, in order to move up the corporate ladder. Across the board, employees, be they male or female, with "flexible" partners are better able to take advantage of opportunities for advancement.

Employers' expectations of constant availability create one of the biggest constraints that workers confront. We want to emphasize that these issues are by no means limited to employees with children. They extend to all those who have care obligations at home. As we noted in chapter 3, the time commitment expectations of employers have ramped up dramatically in the past few decades, especially in the managerial, technical, and professional occupations. The improvements in high-speed Internet access and developments in technologies such as Blackberries and iPhones have contributed to increased employer and client expectations for twenty-four-hour availability. While many find the technology to be liberating because it allows for more flexibility in where one works, the overall result has been a blurring of the boundaries between home and work.

Travel requirements create another important structural constraint. While one might expect that technological innovations would decrease the need for travel, in our globalizing economy, the reverse is true. The connections made possible by new technology expand business networks and multiply the destinations required for business travel.[20] Therefore, business travel is on the rise, despite—or actually because of—these dramatic improvements in information technology.

One man, an engineer whose wife left her job as a nurse to stay home with their children, described trips to Germany, China, and Brazil. He noted that nowadays employees on all rungs of the ladder have to travel for their jobs. The global nature of today's companies means that you cannot stay under the radar or rise above it.

To compound matters, employers also may expect their employees to travel on short notice, without regard to family concerns. And travel is one of the most difficult variables for workers with children (or other caregiving responsibilities) to manage. If your boss tells you on Friday that you need to leave for China on Sunday morning, someone has to be available at a moment's notice to provide twenty-four-hour care for the children. And, ironically, as one woman told us, travel can be the specific attribute that can attract a person to a job during one phase of her life and drive her out of the workforce during another phase: "I took on a job with a lot of international travel and did not realize until I actually had kids of my own how hard this would be. Travel was an original enticement to the job and [is] now one of the worse parts. My mother always worked, and so combining job and family was a given assumption. It's just that some jobs are harder than others." This woman's experience reinforces the notion that the world of work is changing, and that the struggles between work and gender are keenly fueled by the new and changing conditions in which we all live.

Beyond travel for work, job transfers to new locations—domestically but especially internationally—have a big impact on a family's work situation. And they are a distinctive feature of the twenty-first-century workforce. The *New York Times* notes that more than five million men and women, nearly four percent of the U.S. workforce, move each year for work-related reasons—to a new job after a layoff, to higher-paying work, or to the next rung in a career.[21] The *Times* reported in June 2008, "It's common for couples to place more emphasis on the man's career, according to a 2007 study of more than nine thousand married men and women ages twenty-five to fifty-nine. The researchers, from the University of Iowa and the University of California–Davis, also found that when couples relocate, the husband tends to get a salary boost—$3,000 on average. But the wife loses $750."[22]

Moving to a new part of the country can also precipitate the exit of one member of a dual-income household from the labor force. Many women we spoke with described how they moved to accommodate their husband's opportunity for job advancement in another city. With the expectation of "getting the kids settled in" and then finding a new job, these women found it challenging to go back to a high-powered job without contacts in a new city. One woman we interviewed, who had left a corporate executive position and moved for her husband's job, found his new travel schedule was unpredictable. She couldn't find an appropriate child care situation, and they lacked an extended family network in the new city. These factors contributed to her decision not to seek a new job after the move. She describes her transition to stay-at-home parenthood as "involuntary." If they had stayed in their original location, she would have remained at work. As one woman put it, "I was the 'silent partner' in a corporate transfer, i.e., he moved toward a job, I left a job behind and found none to go to."

Moving internationally introduces a whole new set of variables with which to contend. Setting up house when moving from New Jersey to Minnesota is nothing compared to setting up house when moving from New Jersey to Hong Kong. One woman living abroad told us, "I consider raising my children and caring for my family as my 'work.' It is very much a full-time occupation and, due to the fact that [we] live and work overseas, is essential to the functioning of our household." Another woman told us, "I worked part-time in my field while I earned my MA. My husband is now pursuing an MPA in London, UK. Thus, I left my part-time job and moved to London. I am currently seeking a job in my field. Had this not happened, I would have stayed at my former job (which I loved) while applying to nonprofit orgs in New York (of which there are many). In London, my prospects are considerably narrower and I struggle with concerns that I will not get a job within my field within a reasonable amount of time, and that I will become less employable in my field the longer I go without a job in my field." Beyond the logistics of resettling that can require the full attention of one parent, a spouse's ability to work can be further diminished by legal issues surrounding work permits. Several women we surveyed reported that "not having a work permit and living in a foreign country limited opportunities."

Of course, some women are able to keep their jobs in these circumstances by arranging to "work from home" and telecommute. These women strike creative agreements with their bosses to allow them to maintain their professional life. These types of jobs, however, are not the norm, and few women are able to make these types of deals with their employers when faced with a major relocation.

Avoiding Bias

Many employers have instituted a variety of flexible work options for their employees, including telecommuting, flexible hours, part-time work options, job sharing, and paid parenting leave. Workers with caregiving responsibilities value the idea of these work options as they, in principle, would allow employees to balance their career and family obligations. Unfortunately, the policies that exist "on the books" are not always what they appear to be.

In some circumstances, the ideal worker norm of complete commitment to work conflicts with caregiving roles. Women who have managed to shatter glass ceilings then hit the maternal wall. They desire the flexibility offered by these policies, but are concerned that by using flexible work options they will be perceived as uncommitted to their careers. These women fear the repercussions of violating the ideal worker norm, and thus engage in what economist Robert Drago terms "bias avoidance," or actions that minimize perceived or actual interference of family obligations on work commitments. Drago's research on faculty members in U.S. colleges and universities found that women were more likely than men to engage in bias avoidance behaviors, such as not requesting a reduced teaching load when needed, missing important events in their children's lives, and coming back to work too soon after childbirth. These women professors reported that they engaged in bias avoidance because they did not want to appear less than committed to their jobs.[23] The women we interviewed were frank about their bias avoidance. One executive put it this way: "The women, we learned to say 'I have an appointment at three,' but you would never say I have to pick up my daughter and take her to the doctor. Camouflage. You just didn't emphasize that. You would just use euphemisms for that part of it. That was the shorthand that we used. I learned from my customers who were professional women with children." Another woman told us, "I never admitted to any kind of issues with child care at all at work. I really did pretend I was just like any other man that way, that there weren't any child issues."

A nationally representative survey of highly educated women found that even when their employers offered flexible work opportunities, tacit rules prevented them from taking advantage of the offerings. Only four out of ten of the women whose firms offered telecommuting policies felt that they were actually able to take them. The stigma attached to part-time positions at the senior level was fairly even across fields, with just over one-third of lawyers, doctors, and businesswomen reporting barriers to moving to a part-time position. Women in banking and finance, however, look strikingly different. Three-quarters of the women in the financial sector reported serious barriers to taking a part-time position.[24]

Even women at the highest levels of corporate leadership report that while 91 percent can be flexible if needed for family reasons, only 24 percent believe they can turn down an opportunity at work for family reasons without harming their career trajectory. And a mere 15 percent of these corporate leaders believe they can take advantage of any type of flexible work opportunity, including a parental leave or sabbatical, without negative repercussions for their careers.[25] A female managing director at Bankers Trust describes the stigma in the following way: "Women who work part-time are often treated differently. . . . When you are on a flexible schedule, you aren't considered part of the regular workforce. People can assume that you don't want a career or that you don't care as much about moving forward."[26]

Lacy, a product manager for a major bank, relayed the difficulty she had negotiating with her boss about going part-time, which was a flexible work option offered by the bank. "When I cut my hours my boss said he'd pay me less per hour [than I was currently making]. After three months of fighting and going several levels above him, I was able to keep my hourly wage. He was reluctant to let me go part-time at all." Although Lacy won her fight to reduce her hours without a wage reduction, she found that as she worked fewer hours, she was assigned less-important projects. As the assignments became less interesting, her desire to remain at the bank waned. Eventually, Lacy decided to leave her job.

Unbeknownst to Lacy, at the same time that she was fighting to keep her wage, an engineer at a technology research company had taken a similar case to court. Linda Lovell argued that under the Equal Pay Act, she should be paid the same hourly rate as her full-time male co-worker. In 2003, a Virginia court ruled that employers have to base pay on the actual job and required training, and could not justify paying differential wages solely on the basis of a reduced schedule. In other words, the court ruled in favor of equal compensation (on a prorated basis) for full- and part-time work in the same job.[27]

Throughout this chapter we have focused primarily on women, but these problems are not only faced by women. Men, too, can face a so-called maternal wall with regard to their parental responsibilities. Likewise, even those who don't have children may have living parents, and the care needs of that generation are growing rapidly. These issues are not only women's issues. Rather, anyone with caregiving responsibilities, whether for an aging parent, an ailing family member, or a child, can face many of the same obstacles. Indeed, the "maternal wall" can be construed more broadly as a "caregiver wall."

We have explored in this chapter the ways that tacit and explicit discrimination on the job affect professional women's lives. In the following chapters, we turn our attention to the pressures of home-based responsibilities, and how these pressures also shape women's relationship to work.

CHAPTER FIVE

Second Shift Redux

I can put the wash on the line,
feed the kids, get dressed,
pass out the kisses
and get to work by five to nine.

ENJOLI PERFUME COMMERCIAL, 1970S

The more time couples spend at work, the less time they have to run the household. And, as we've noted earlier in our discussion of 100-hour couples, time is a particularly scarce resource for busy families. Competing with the demands of work, a major drain on women's time is what sociologist Arlie Hochschild calls the second shift—the work women do to maintain and sustain the household in addition to their paid employment.[1] Here she gives life to the old adage, "A man may work from sun to sun, but a woman's work is never done." Women shoulder a disproportionate share of housework, and this second shift acts as a significant stressor for women across socioeconomic groups.

While women have made significant gains in the workplace itself, the gender division of labor at home endures. And even while husbands contribute more to tasks at home now than ever before, the primary responsibility for running the household among married couples with children continues to rest with women. A recent trend to hire household help is opening possibilities to redefine this aspect of women's lives, but even when families hire people to watch their children or clean their homes, women tend to take on the burden of managing the work that is done in the home and the care of the children.

As such, mothers feel the pressure of managing their homes and families along with long hours at work, and as we've noted, one response for many of these women is to downsize or quit their jobs. Women's professional lives can be derailed by unequal burdens of housework (or management of household staff), husband's travel schedule, husband's mobility, and the need to care for family members who are ill or aging. This chapter analyzes the ways in which care in these private spheres pressures women to reduce, reorient, or resign their jobs.

Gender and Housework

Hochschild argued that as married mothers entered the workforce at a record pace, their household responsibilities did not necessarily diminish. For many of the women she studied, this second shift led to exhaustion, depression, and more-frequent illness. Some, who criticize Hochschild's work from the late 1980s as out of date, perceive that men contribute far more time to household tasks than they did when she conducted her study.[2] Yet current statistics confirm that while men *do* spend more time now on tasks at home, women continue to shoulder the burden of household work. One woman we surveyed summed up these sentiments in the following manner:

> My job is very flexible and also very demanding. I have many opportunities to do consulting and research work outside my main employment which provide career development but are often stressful. I find myself working nights, weekends, and early mornings to stay caught up. Even with the extra work I do, I am perpetually behind and pulled in multiple directions. Many of my colleagues say the same thing. We hire out what we can but suffer unreasonable expectations at home, at work, and among extended families. Parents and other relatives wish us to be traditionally available to provide support and free labor. Although all the women in our extended families work full-time jobs we are expected to prepare food for family functions, decorate, invite, be gracious, and clean up. Sadly, that's only one

example of the expectations which challenge us to "balance." I have dozens more.

Clean Up, Clean Up, Everybody Clean Up

Time spent on household tasks has changed remarkably little since the early 1900s. Technology has sped up the process of washing clothes, cooking meals, and washing dishes, yet families spend a considerable amount of time cleaning house, shopping, caring for children, and doing laundry. Washing machines and dryers reduce time per load of laundry, but now people have a higher expectation for clean clothes, so laundry is done more often. Increases in time spent on housecleaning can be explained by a higher standard of cleanliness (and larger houses).[3] While the number of children per family has fallen, the time spent with each child has risen. Women spend less time on housework than previous generations, and men spend more than their predecessors. But still, women bear the brunt of household chores.

In 2006, employed married women with children under the age of six did 62 percent of the housework, spending an average of thirty-five hours per week on household tasks, as opposed to the twenty-one hours per week devoted by their employed husbands.[4] As their children get older, the time spent on household activities by both mothers and fathers declines. When the youngest child is between six and seventeen, the number of hours spent on household tasks falls to twenty-eight and eighteen hours per week, for mothers and fathers, respectively. Still the ratio stays fairly constant, at 60 percent for moms and 40 percent for dads.

Even married mothers who work full-time do two-thirds of the housework and child care, and this is approximately 1.8 times as much as full-time employed married men.[5] Another study found that two-thirds of highly educated, employed women report taking time off to take a child to the doctor, for example, as opposed to 7 percent of their husbands. Women with children were so used to the pressures of having to bend their job to the family's needs during their workweek, they even had a term for days when family responsibilities impinged on work time: "compromise days." To further compound the issue, four out of ten women report that they feel that their husbands actually generate more work than they contribute to household tasks.[6]

Nevertheless, men *have* increased their housework contributions significantly over the past few decades. In 1965, married women who worked full-time spent six times as many hours as their husbands on household tasks. Predictably, when women are out of the workforce they spend significantly more hours on housework. Married, at-home mothers with children under the age of six spend fifty-five hours per week on household activities, and those whose youngest child is between six and seventeen report spending forty-eight hours per week on household tasks.

While women are working far more hours at home than their husbands, men's hours outpace women's hours at their paid employment. So women and men "work" very similar total hours. Employed parents with children under the age of six work the most total hours (including household and work activities) at sixty-nine and seventy hours, respectively, for fathers and mothers. Parents of older children work slightly less at sixty-five and sixty-four hours, respectively. In their nonwork time, employed married women with children sleep about half an hour more per night than their husbands, but the men enjoy about 45 more minutes of leisure time per day than their wives.

When we examine the division of labor at home more closely, it quickly becomes evident that household chores are typically gendered. Researchers have found that household work is highly segregated by gender, with wives still primarily doing so-called women's work.[7] Sociologist Theodore Greenstein reports that women do roughly three-quarters of traditionally female tasks, such as cooking and laundry, while men perform about 70 percent of traditionally male tasks, such as lawn mowing and car maintenance.[8] In our survey sample, for example, women were more likely to report doing the majority of the cooking, laundry, grocery shopping, and bill paying. They reported that their husbands were more likely to manage investments, as well as to maintain the lawn and vehicles.

They also reported sharing equally the responsibility of doing dishes and walking the dog (or other pet care). Housecleaning was divided fairly evenly among the women doing the work primarily alone (31 percent), splitting it equally with their spouses (34 percent), and paying someone to come in and clean (29 percent). Only 3 percent reported that their husbands assumed the primary responsibility for cleaning the home.

Even though men nowadays devote more time to household tasks than their fathers, they typically spend time on tasks that can be done on a weekly, or more sporadic basis, such as lawn and car maintenance. Men are less likely to be doing the daily chores of cooking and laundry. The more intermittent nature of these tasks gives men greater control over when they make their contributions. So, while it is true that men today are more amenable to housework than their dads, they still have not approached parity with their wives. While children, as they age, can increasingly contribute to household tasks, it remains that parents, and in particular mothers, with children at home spend more time on household tasks than couples in child-free households. In other words, children create more work than they offset by doing chores around the house.

Some argue that this division of household labor is unfair to women. That question aside, the unequal burden can have economic repercussions as well. The time a woman spends on housework appears to be directly related to the amount of money she earns in the labor market. A recent study found that for each $7,500 increase in earnings, women decrease time spent on housework by about an hour per week.[9] This finding suggests that women's increased purchasing power enables them to outsource some of their household tasks for others to perform.[10] Studies have also shown that spending more time on housework reduces women's wages, with a two percent reduction for each additional ten hours spent on housework.[11] But it remains unclear whether doing housework lowers wages. It may be that women with lower wages are willing to do more housework or less willing to spend money to outsource. Alternatively, it may be that women who spend more time on housework have less energy and therefore are less productive in the workforce and thus earn lower wages.[12] In all likelihood, both arguments contribute to a full explanation. Women who earn lower wages may be willing to do more housework, which in turn lowers the energy level remaining for market work.

Outsourcing as a Solution to the Second Shift?

Regardless of the reason, however, it is clear that as women's wages rise, they are increasingly able to outsource household tasks, and the market has kept pace with these shifts. In 2006, for instance, the Web site Care.com was launched, and now serves over thirty-three cities. It offers one-stop shopping for those seeking care and tutoring for their children, someone to clean their home, a person to walk the dog, or even a companion for Grandma.

Still, even the outsourcing of household tasks requires time and effort. Someone must order the take-out meals, shop for groceries online, and manage child care, housecleaning and laundry services. Frequently, the burden of that management falls to the wife. In our survey sample, for instance, women were the primary managers of household help, excluding lawn and car maintenance. Among the women we interviewed, hiring and supervising this care was a major stressor, and this stress came from myriad angles.

On one level, women reported being beleaguered by the legal and administrative aspects of managing someone to care for their children. Many remember President Bill Clinton's first two unsuccessful nominations for Attorney General, Zoë Baird and Kimba Wood. Both women were derailed in their bids to become the first female U.S. Attorney General when it came to light that both had previously employed undocumented immigrants as nannies. Another recent start-up company, Collegenannies.com, operating in more than seventeen states, seeks to eliminate that particular stressor from families' lives, by assuming the role of employer and thereby take on responsibility to "ensure the employee is legal to work, covered by workers' compensation insurance, liability insurance, specific auto insurance (most homeowners and auto insurance does not cover employees), [and ensure] payroll forms are processed, and payroll taxes are properly withheld."[13] Unless they use such a service, families who hire someone to care for their children in their own home are saddled with these responsibilities.

Beyond these administrative tasks, many women are uncomfortable with other aspects of outsourcing care. One woman noted that she struggled with ethical concerns in terms of doing what was "fair and right" by her nanny. Another described a situation in which her husband was out of town for work, and she needed to be in court. The nanny called and said she didn't feel well that day, but the mother leaned on her to come to work anyway. Social critic Barbara Ehrenreich and sociologist Arlie Hochschild expose yet another dimension of this issue by noting that "in the absence of help from their male partners, many women have made it in tough 'male world' careers only by turning over the care of their children, elderly parents, and homes to women from the Third World."[14] Ehrenreich and Hochschild argue that one of the problematic ethical undercurrents in relying on "imported" care is that the care providers are often leaving their own children behind in the care of others, and may not even get to see their own children for years at a time. Outsourcing of care is, therefore, not just a straightforward financial transaction.

Home as Women's Domain

Other mothers we interviewed pointed to society's role in perpetuating the expectation that women shoulder the brunt of household tasks. After years of working 70-plus hours per week at a start-up company, Kate felt that she and her husband had hit the wall. Realizing that they could not sustain the 140-hour couple lifestyle they were living, they decided that one of them would ratchet back on the career front and relieve the other's obligations to "cover" the kids. They tried to calculate how much more he would earn if he could invest 100 percent in his career and she pulled back, as well as how much she would earn if the roles were reversed. They decided that this was a decision that couldn't be made just by looking at a financial spreadsheet. Kate would never be able to fully extricate herself from the household responsibilities in the same way that he could, she said,

> because no matter what, as the wife, even if you're working full-time, you're still the one who's making dinner. [My husband] was invested 70 percent in career and 30 percent trying to cover for the times he needed to be there when I wasn't there. When we took the 30 percent burden off of him, and he could invest closer to 100 percent into his career, the return was very high. We weren't convinced that would be true for me because no matter what, the pediatrician's calling me, the school's calling me. The mother is the first line of contact, unless you specify clearly to call the father. We set it up that way, society set it up that way.

Women as Caregivers

Sometimes the stress related to health issues of a child, parent, or sibling leads women to leave their positions in the workforce. We interviewed women who described how they had expected to remain in their jobs, but had to reconsider when confronted with a health problem. One former pension fund manager, now at home, said she always had intended to work, even after her children were born. "Never in a million years did I imagine I would be a stay-at-home parent," she said. But while she was pregnant with her first baby, her father fell terminally ill and her sister was diagnosed with cancer. The bulk of the responsibility for caregiving fell on her shoulders. She felt that she couldn't manage working in such a high-pressure job and manage her family's health care needs at the same time.

Just as women usually have primary responsibility for children, they are also often charged with the care of other, especially elderly, family members. Sometimes called the "sandwich generation," these women are responsible for the care of children on one hand and parents on the other. We examine the sandwich generation phenomenon further in chapter 8.

Informal caregiving, loosely defined as unpaid care or financial support provided by family or friends to someone with a disability or chronic illness, often falls on the shoulders of women. A critical source of long-term care in the United States, the Older Women's League estimates that almost one-quarter of households provide informal care to a friend or relative over the age of fifty.[15] The typical informal caregiver is a married, employed woman in her midforties.[16] Indeed, informal caregiving is a highly gendered task. Adult American women can expect to spend up to eighteen years helping an aging parent, and almost one-third will care for both elders and children at the same time.[17]

Providing care to an extended family member can present different challenges than care for young children.[18] Informal caregiving of elderly or disabled family members is more unpredictable than child care. The need for informal care may be intermittent or continuous, and the type of care may require daily physical contact and direct care or management of other health care providers. Female caregivers spend more time and provide a higher level of care than men do, and women are more likely to report high stress (4 or 5 on a 5-point scale) associated with caregiving than men.[19]

Adding caregiving for an aging parent to the already hectic life of a full-time working parent can be the event that tips a woman out of the workforce, or prompts her to shift her career priorities by forgoing a promotion or otherwise stepping off the "fast track" at work. In fact, a recent study estimates that women who begin to provide informal care have a 50 percent likelihood of dropping out of the labor force.[20] In our survey sample, 12 percent of the women who indicated that they at some point had taken at least six months off from work, did so in order to care for a family member other than a child. Given societal demographics, we can expect increasing pressures on women who are trying to balance work, raising a family, and caring for parents at the same time.

The More Things Change, the More They Stay the Same

Many of the women we interviewed were surprised that, despite achievements in school and on the job, they still ended up bearing the primary burden of household responsibilities. Having seen themselves as "just as smart and capable and experienced" as their male peers and having married what they thought were like-minded men, they were not expecting to shoulder the load at home. This is illustrated in Margo's experience. She met her husband, Alex, at an Ivy League business school, and they both worked many long hours in the private equity industry. She recalls thinking before her child was born that since she and her husband were professional equals—earning similar salaries and holding similar jobs—they would share equally in housework tasks. And, as busy professionals, they did, for a while.

Margo, however, describes the arrival of their daughter as "a wake-up call." Once Margo returned to work after having the baby, she felt she had to make accommodations to be home by six o'clock each night. She noticed, though, that Alex had not made many changes to his daily routine. At that time he was traveling internationally up to two weeks each month, so most of the child care fell to her. She was surprised that once she became a mother, she no longer experienced the equality that had characterized her marriage before children.

Now in her late thirties, Margo continues to work full-time. In order to balance her family responsibilities and the work that she loves, she now telecommutes from her home in Chicago and works most days from 8:00 a.m. to 4:00 p.m. She works fewer hours than before the children were born, while Alex now works more hours. His job requires him to be away from home four to five nights per week. Margo accepts that her husband is not going to contribute as much as she would have liked to child care and household tasks. Another woman summed up the experiences of Margo and so many other women by noting that she and her husband now joke around about how "mainstream we ended up looking" through the gender roles they each assume.

Men today certainly perform more household tasks than they did twenty years ago. Nevertheless, this chapter illustrates that women continue to shoulder the responsibility of keeping the household running. This prevalence of the second shift adds significant stressors for women and can lead them to reduce or even quit their jobs. In the following chapter, we focus our attention on one particular aspect of the second shift: arranging and managing child care when both parents are at their jobs.

∿∿∿∿∿∿∿∿∿∿∿∿∿∿∿∿∿∿∿∿∿∿∿∿∿∿∿∿∿∿∿∿∿∿∿∿

CHAPTER SIX

Child Care Dilemmas

Cry, baby bunting,
Father's gone a-hunting,
Mother's gone a-milking,
Sister's gone a-silking,
And brother's gone to buy a skin
To wrap the baby bunting in.

ENGLISH POEM, 1784

∿∿∿∿∿∿∿∿∿∿∿∿∿∿∿∿∿∿∿∿∿∿∿∿∿∿∿∿∿∿∿∿∿∿∿∿∿∿

How American society configures the relationships among mothers, fathers, and children tells us something important about how our culture shapes gender, work, and identity. While biology determines the reality that women give birth, it is our culture that situates mothers as the principal caretakers and companions of young children.[1] While individuals may buck these norms, they often find they are swimming against the current. Jane, a twenty-six-year veteran in the field of child care and the director of a child development center we interviewed for this study, told us that while she has noticed more interest and involvement on the part of dads in child care issues, moms continue to play the dominant role. This cultural norm of women's role as primary caregiver collides with the competing role of ideal worker. The key issue in all of this is who, how, when, and where the kids are cared for while mom is at work. Struggles over how to negotiate this dilemma surfaced as a key concern for women we interviewed. In some cases, the child care dilemma resulted in women quitting their jobs or downsizing their careers.

As working moms ourselves, we do not intend to say that combining children and careers cannot be done. On the contrary, as documented in chapter 4, many women find viable ways to combine paid work with raising children. Some couples are able to share child care responsibilities between themselves. Others have the advantage of extended family members who assist with caring for the children. And still others manage to find nonrelative care options that fit their family's needs and budget. Some families are quite satisfied with how child care fits into their lives and think their children benefit in terms of practice at social interaction, problem solving, and self-sufficiency skills. Unfortunately, however, as we heard from many of the women we interviewed who are working or who have left their jobs to be at-home moms, many families continue to struggle with reliable, long-term solutions to their child care dilemmas.

Women we interviewed described how even when resolved to work, finding someone to care for their children created a significant barrier to employment. In this chapter, we focus on the structural obstacles that create these difficulties, namely the mismatch between the availability of acceptable and affordable care options and the child care needs of working families. This mismatch between care options and workplace demands is central to understanding the phenomenon of women reducing or resigning from their careers.

Why Is Child Care a Barrier?

Why do so many women at all income levels say that securing suitable child care presents a barrier to employment? The simple answer is that for many families, good quality, affordable child care is not available when and where they need it. Sometimes the care is available, but expensive. Often, even the expensive, high-quality care is not available. And even when available and affordable, the hours provided may not meet the needs of workers, especially dual-career parents. The modern workplace imposes demands on workers outside of a traditional nine-to-five workday, and these demands often collide with child care arrangements that conform to this schedule (in part so the child care workers can get home to care for their own children).

Parents want high-quality care for their children, in a convenient location, that offers flexibility in the daily schedule. Parents want to leave their children in a clean, safe, and nurturing environment, preferably close to their homes or their workplaces. They desire low child-teacher ratios, qualified teachers, and the option of dropping off their children before, or picking them up after, standard working hours. The mismatch between what parents want and what is available for child care can be seen in terms of available "slots," the quality of care, costs, and schedule.

All of this stands in stark contrast to the child care options available to families. Jane, the child development center director, remarked, "The industry is slow growing." She went on to note that "low pay, few benefits, high turnover, little respect, and the fact that males who attempt to enter the field face bias" are all reasons for this slow growth, despite the demand from working parents.

As a result, there is a serious shortage of licensed child care slots. For example, the National Child Care Resource and Referral Agency reports that the working mothers of 11.3 million children under the age of five regularly use some kind of child care. At the same time, only 10.8 million legally operating slots exist, including those for school-age children.[2] The shortages are apparent across the country. In 2006, licensed child care was available for only 27 percent of California children under the age of fourteen.[3] In Minnesota, only thirty licensed child care slots exist for every one hundred children under the age of six with working parents.[4] According to the U.S. Department of Defense, even given great strides to increase child care capacity for military families, in 2006 there remained an estimated shortage of 27,000 child care spaces for the U.S. military.[5] And this situation is even worse for low-income families who have to get on long waiting lists for child care subsidies.

Jane also spoke to the continuing gap between the need for quality care and available spots: "Right now we have 294 kids on our list. The list usually ranges from a high of about 350 to a low of about 275. Shortly before we opened the new building we topped out at about 425 kids, and we haven't dropped below 230 kids in at least six years. There are many factors that can impact the length of time a family waits, but it would be safe to say that most families wait at least 18–20 months and often much more." Therefore, even when high-quality care, such as that which Jane's center provides, exists, the length of time parents must wait to have their children admitted often far exceeds the leaves women can negotiate with their employer.

QUALITY OF CARE

When child care slots are available, they are often not of high quality. In Jane's words, "any decent program is going to have a waiting list." Typical indicators of quality include low child-to-staff ratios, qualified teachers, low staff turnover, and, of course, safety. In addition, high-quality caregivers are caring and attentive, understand and employ age-appropriate child development practices, and can communicate well with parents. In contrast, low-quality caregivers have responsibility for too many children, and often are hired under the premise that the primary qualification for caring for children is simply to be a present adult.[6] And the pay scale for child care workers reflects these minimal qualifications for the job. For example, salaries at one highly regarded child development center attached to a university, whose staff all had college degrees and decades of experience, ranged from $28,000 to a maximum of $34,000. So, well-qualified, dedicated, experienced child care workers (as certainly exist) are not in it for the money.

Studies have shown that the typical day care center in the United States provides only mediocre quality. Jane observed, "You can warehouse kids anywhere." The Cost, Quality, and Outcomes Study, conducted in the mid-1990s, rated child care centers according to two well-regarded measures of child quality, the Early Childhood Environmental Rating Scale and the Infant-Toddler Environment Rating Scale.[7] On average, the child care centers were rated about halfway between "minimal" and "good." The researchers found high variability across regions, with centers in the Northeast and in California outperforming centers in the South. They also found variation within states, depending on the type of child care center investigated: nonprofit centers were typically rated higher than for-profit centers, and preschool classrooms outperformed infant and toddler rooms.[8] Studies of relative care and nonrelative care in a family setting, or what we refer to as family-based child care, are not as common, but one that used similar rating scales found that family-based child care arrangements were, on average, similar in quality to centers.[9]

HANDING OVER A THIRD (OR MORE) OF YOUR PAYCHECK

Child care is expensive. And, as we noted earlier, children are the sole responsibility of parents until they are school age, when society begins to contribute by funding public schools, and so these costs are borne almost exclusively by individual families. In the United States, a parent of an infant can expect to pay anywhere from $4,020 to $14,225 per year for full-time center-based care, depending on where they live. Fees for older preschoolers are slightly lower, running on average from $3,900 to $10,200.[10] Families in Connecticut, for example, pay over $11,000 per year for infant center-based care, and more than $8,700 for the same infant in family-based care. The same arrangements in Ohio would be considerably lower at just over $6,600 for center-based and just under $6,000 for family-based infant care.[11] In Minneapolis-Saint Paul, a family with one preschooler and one infant enrolled in full-time center care can expect to pay about $24,000 annually for child care, and would pay $15,045 for family-based child care. (These numbers decline to $16,000 and $12,000 in greater Minnesota.) To help put this in perspective, full tuition plus fees for the 2008–9 school year at the University of Minnesota is $10,272.[12]

MAKING THE SCHEDULE WORK

While the costs and quality of child care are important to families, it seems that finding the right kind of care at the right times presents a larger barrier to families searching for care. In a 2007 survey of Minnesota parents, for example, 29 percent reported that the child care costs are too high, and 15 percent cited a lack of quality child care. But 44% of Minnesota parents surveyed reported that finding the preferred type, schedule, or location of care presented a major barrier to securing acceptable child care.[13] Many parents have to cobble together different types of care to cover the child care time that they need. For example, the National Association of Child Care Resource and Referral Agencies reports that one-fourth of children under the age of five whose mothers work report using multiple child care arrangements.

As we mentioned above, even when they are able to secure a slot, many mothers cited the inflexibility of the hours of care as barriers to employment. With modern workplaces expecting workers to be able to work late on short notice, the rigid opening and closing times of many child care settings places enormous stress on dual-career parents. Many centers and family-based day care providers charge by the minute for late pickups, and will call child protection services if the parent is one hour late. The collision of workplace demands for overtime and rigid child care hours often make it challenging for both partners in a dual-career family to pursue their careers fully.

A final dimension of the timing of care is getting a spot in the first place. Above, we discussed the relationship between waiting lists for child care slots and quality. Securing a spot for your child before your maternity leave runs out presents another problem related to waiting lists. Few women we interviewed were able to synchronize these events, and they ended up scrambling to get some combination of nanny and family coverage until they could secure long-term placement for their child. And, even in the best of circumstances, the lack of available care when working parents need it is a widespread problem. A *New York Times* article focused on problems that Google, the progressive internet-based company, was facing with child care issues: "The wait list ballooned insanely, finally reaching over 700 people. New employees who arrived at Google thinking they were getting in-house day care were stunned to discover that it could take up to two years to land a coveted spot."[14]

Explaining the Gap

Why is it so challenging for working parents to find suitable care for their children? If the demand for such care exists, we would expect that market forces would lead to increased supply. In fact, if the child care market were functioning properly, as more women entered the workforce and the demand for care rose, we would expect to see the number of slots supplied increase. As child care employers expand their capacity, the working conditions and wages for child care workers should rise. Presumably the child care employers could invest in better-quality buildings and supplies, and perhaps more important, with increased wages, the employers could attract and retain higher-quality workers. Of course, the price of care would rise concomitantly, but only up to the point where the demand for and supply of high-quality child care slots would be equal, and at this point, economists would say that the market for child care would clear. But observation tells us that the market does not clear. In fact there are real shortages of high-quality care.

Here's where the system breaks down. When parents (mothers) are faced with the decision to return to work, they need to compare the value of their earnings and the value of the time at home that they give up to go to work. The value of spending time at home includes the value of leisure, plus the value of any goods or services that they would produce if they remained at home. Care for children is most likely the highest-valued good or service that has to be purchased when a parent returns to work. Since, on average, women earn less than their husbands, it is usually (but not always) the case that the mother's salary (i.e., what she gains by going to work) is compared against the cost of purchasing outside child care. So if the price of child care exceeds the mother's salary, the mother may choose to remain home rather than return to her job and place her child in care. She determines that the value of the care she gives her children exceeds the value of the earnings that she forgoes in the labor market.

Some of the women we interviewed felt their salaries were not sufficient to pay for child care. One woman commented that she thought she might like to return to work, but that with three small children, she couldn't earn enough to cover the child care expenses. A nurse with one child in day care reflected on her ability to remain employed if she decides to have more children: "For us, we're at a point where as our family grows, using day care won't be financially viable. . . . At this point . . . we pay for day care and I still make more than enough to contribute to our household, but you know if we have two or three kids it would be ridiculous to be paying fully for day care."

One problem with this way of thinking is that it does not account for the long-term effects on earning capacity. It may be that a mother's earnings are less than the cost of the child care, in a given period of time. But as children grow older, their child care needs diminish to eventually zero. After that time, women who took time off to care for children return to work with a significant wage penalty. Therefore, it may be that on a purely financial basis, it actually would make sense in the long run for her to work and pay for the child care.[15] Presumably her husband's income could cover whatever child care costs hers could not. The children are half his, after all.

Regardless, when faced with the dilemmas of child care, it is difficult to take this long-term view. For most people, the price they are willing to pay for child care is capped by the income of the lower-earning spouse, usually the mother. As we've illustrated through examples in previous chapters, parents' decisions about whose career will bend to the needs of the children cannot be tallied neatly on a spreadsheet. And when you factor in the social pressure on moms to act as principal caretakers and companions of young children and the continuing stigmatization of dads who assume these roles, the conditions under which individuals make "choices" are clarified.

From a purely financial perspective, though, economists have estimated the connection between the price of child care and a mother's willingness to be employed. Economist David Blau, for example, estimated that a 1 percent increase in a mother's wage leads to a 0.17 percent increase in the likelihood that she will be employed. So an increase in a mother's wage from fifteen dollars per hour to twenty-five dollars per hour would increase the likelihood of her working by 11.3 percent. Similarly, he found that mothers' employment is sensitive to changes in the price of child care. For every 10 percent increase in the price, mothers are 2 percent less likely to work.[16] In sum, research shows that as mothers' wages rise, they are more likely to work and are more likely to use paid center care for their children. Additionally, a decrease in the price of child care increases the quantity of child care demanded, and it also increases the employment rate of mothers.

Therefore, the price of child care, of any quality, can only rise so much, and that increase is capped by the incomes of the parents (usually mothers). High-quality care is expensive, and the biggest contributor to the cost is labor. Nationally, almost 80 percent of the costs of running a nonprofit child care center go into labor.[17] In order to attract high-quality workers, centers need to pay high wages. The average earnings of child care workers in 2006 were $9.05 per hour or $18,820 annually. The bottom line is that if families won't pay higher prices, centers can't afford to hire higher-quality workers.

So, How Do We Fix This?

Given that the cost of child care is constrained by mothers' incomes, it seems that the only way to solve the problem is to increase our subsidization of child care, and that subsidization could be generated publicly, through government intervention, and privately, through employer provision of child care benefits. Studies show that child care subsidization increases female employment and productivity.[18] In addition, high-quality early childhood education offers extremely high returns to society in terms of a better educated workforce for the future.[19] These changes benefit both the firm and society at large. Moreover, if we believe that children are public goods, not pets, then there is an argument for government subsidization of child care.

Child care subsidization is precisely the solution many other countries have adopted. The Nordic countries, for instance, offer publicly provided child care at subsidized prices, and studies show that these policies lead to increases in female employment.[20] The United States currently subsidizes child care for working parents, but in far lesser amounts than do Nordic countries.[21] France provides some subsidization of care for children under three, and free universal preschool for all children between the ages of three and six, when they enroll in kindergarten.[22] These represent just two of the models that different countries have adopted.

Many advocates in the United States have been pushing for greater access to early childhood education. As one example, Arthur Rolnick, senior vice president and director of research at the Federal Reserve Bank of Minneapolis, undertook a major campaign to raise public awareness of the incredibly high returns offered by early childhood education. Thanks largely to his efforts to educate business leaders of the high potential returns on their investments, the private, business-backed Minnesota Early Learning Foundation was created in 2006 and to date has raised $4.5 million for early childhood education. Although still operating on a relatively small scale, this effort provides a model that could be expanded to a national scale, given the political will to do so.

In addition to seeing the long-term economic benefits of high-quality early childhood education, firms might also be convinced to subsidize child care in order to increase the productivity of their workforce today. Improved worker performance, as well as reduced turnover and absenteeism, are among the positive benefits reported by employers who offer these types of direct child care benefits. Also, because employers do not pay employment taxes on benefits, firms can reduce their tax burden by casting some of an employee's compensation as a child care subsidy.[23] As an added bonus to the employee, these benefits also accrue to workers on a tax-free basis.

While still a small percent of all firms, an increasing number of companies now offer some type of employer-sponsored child care program. The numbers of those that do has grown rapidly. In 1978, the U.S. Department of Labor documented 105 employer-sponsored child care programs; within twenty years that number had ballooned to roughly 8,000.[24] Well-known companies like Cisco Systems and Oracle report a $12,000-a-year average child care subsidy. [25] Clearly firms have begun to see the upside of providing these types of benefits, and we should expect to see this trend continue.

However, there are some downsides to this solution. Jane, the child care director, pointed out that widening the array of on-site child care options can significantly blur the work-life boundaries, and she questions the impact of this on the child. For example, "if your kid has a cold, your boss can now expect you to bring them in and leave them in child care at work. You are trapped now. As a parent, you cannot make a decision to put kids first." She also cautioned that this could mean that parents would not be in a position to shop around for child care that was consistent with their family's values. This was exactly the problem that bedeviled the Google corporation in a well-publicized fight over the kind of in-house child care that Google would provide and subsidize.[26]

And finally, the day when someone writes a chapter on how child care issues affect men's labor force participation will probably signal an end to the problems we describe here. We are noting that child care is a dilemma for women because society conflates the role of giving birth and raising children. Once we disentangle these roles, we open up space to discuss how raising children is a family and societal affair, and not just a "women's issue."

In the following chapters we turn our attention to other reasons women felt pulled toward home and we begin to unpack what women gain when they reduce their work commitments. In the next chapter we delve into the allure of home.

CHAPTER SEVEN

Mama Time

Hey little darlin', your mama's stuck on you
wherever you're going, I'm going there too
bless my child
with the sun in your eyes
and the wings on your shoulders
and the blue in your skies
bless my baby

DEE CARSTENSEN, "BLESS MY CHILD," 2001

Kids can be cranky, demanding, and generally maddening, but there's no feeling in the world like when your two-year-old wraps his arms around your neck and whispers into your ear, "I love you, angel mama." The world stops spinning. Stress melts away. And you are the dead center of that little fellow's world. Unconditional love is intoxicating. And it's hard to conjure up similar moments in the average day at the office.

Being a parent or wanting to be a parent, especially a mother, is at the center of this phenomenon of heading home. The women we interviewed indicated that they *want* to be with their children, even if that involves relying on others to help provide that care some of the time. Many women emphasized that they seek to provide their children with what one woman described as her "version of family life," and some of the women we interviewed found their goal of creating a family life to be at cross-purposes with simultaneously pursuing a demanding career. It's not that they lacked drive or ambition, as is sometimes asserted in discussions of who remains in the labor force, but when push came to shove and given the constraints of their jobs, they made trade-offs. Yet it is also crucial to recognize that this affective dimension of mothering is also deeply cultural. Many women feel they *should* be with their children, and respond to powerful gendered social norms that instill a particular sense of responsibility for caring for their children. Lower tolerance for risk, higher levels of surveillance, and increased expectations for kids' lives to be programmed and scheduled all coalesce to make parenthood a more hands-on affair than it was a generation ago.

And, finally, parenthood is also inextricably bound up with structural issues in society. In the previous chapter, we documented how the economics and the structure of child care options fail to meet the needs of families. Many women feel they *must* be home to provide that care, even if that means pushing the margins of what their family's economic situation will allow. Our discussion up to this point has revolved primarily around the social, political, economic, and demographic forces that shape women's relationship to work, but how do women themselves see their behavior? And what do these actions mean to them? Beyond structural "pushes" from the world of work, what pulls women home?

The Politicization of Spending Time with Your Kids

Here we step into the peculiar politics of spending time with one's kids. The mother-child dyad is one of the most fundamental relationships in our society. Yet when, where, why, and how much time a mother spends with her children is heavily politicized terrain. Whether you are a mom receiving welfare or at the top of your game working as a financial analyst, someone outside of your family probably has an opinion about whether you should be working, and if so, how much. One of the issues here is the naturalizing of gender roles and society's efforts to challenge the reductionistic equation of woman = mother. As a point of departure, to build on a famous quote by anthropologist Margaret Mead, while motherhood is a biological reality, it, like fatherhood, is also a social invention. Many contemporary discussions of women and work deal rather swiftly with the affective dimensions of mothering. These authors tend to offer their own experience as a mother to establish "street creds," before quickly moving to the "real story" beyond women's emotional attachment to mothering.[1] We want to take a closer look at how women frame their feelings about being a parent, because we believe that this perspective is important to understanding broader themes of gender, work, and identity in America. Therefore, while we acknowledge that we are entering a political minefield, it is important to spend some time in this book giving voice to what women we interviewed told us about how *they* saw their role and their experience of being a mother.

Motherhood in the Abstract versus the Real

A few of the women we interviewed, like Karen, a mother of three in her early thirties, foresaw that being a full-on, full-time mom was exactly their calling. "I always wanted to stay home," Karen told us. "From a young age, it is what I wanted to do." About one in five of the women we surveyed indicated that by the time they graduated from college they had anticipated that they would eventually reduce their efforts at work in order to balance work and family. And one-third of those women selected a career that would allow for striking such a balance.

For many more women we interviewed, however, the pull of motherhood toward home was unexpected. This applies both to the moms who have left their jobs and are now at home and to those who are still working and attempting to juggle work and home. And it is to this last category of women who told us, "I didn't aspire to be a mom," that we now turn our attention.

Only one in ten college-educated married women with children we surveyed reported that their family or their intention to have a family influenced their choice of a major in college. And only one in four of these same women who went on to graduate school reported that this was also the case for their graduate studies. Accordingly then, they never anticipated how having children would change their lives and usher in the possibility of becoming an at-home mom.

Therefore, for the majority of women we interviewed, their

strong feelings about being a mom were unanticipated. This finding echoes Mary Ann Mason and Eve Mason Ekman's findings in their study of women negotiating career and family, where they noted that "when women are choosing career directions, the question of marriage and babies is largely abstract."[2] These were women who focused first on career. Few of the women we interviewed saw themselves as "natural" mothers, and for some "just ending up with a family has been a surprise." Some women hadn't contemplated motherhood before they became one and certainly didn't consider motherhood when they were initially setting their educational or career goals. Mason and Ekman attribute this in part to the dramatic rise in age at which women college graduates have their first baby. In 1970, 73 percent of college-educated women had their first baby by thirty, while in 2000, only 36 percent did so in that same time period.[3]

To delve further into this topic, let's start with the case of Lily, a married woman in her midforties and the mother of two children. Lily met her husband, Greg, through mutual friends shortly after finishing college. While they were dating, she completed a master's degree, and soon after they married she decided to go back to school to train to be a college professor. In her early thirties, Lily was en route to a doctorate in philosophy when she found her career plans derailed by what were, for her, unexpected feelings about motherhood. Abandoned by her father to be raised along with her two siblings by a struggling single mother, she was primed from an early age to respond to the imperative that a woman be self-reliant and financially independent. Having helped to raise her own siblings, her feelings about motherhood were shaped by a strong dose of realism and were anything but romanticized. These experiences all contributed to a decided feeling of ambivalence toward children in general. Therefore, she was not prepared for the intensity of feelings she had toward her own children when she had them and how this would prompt her to reprioritize career and family. Lily told us:

> I'm not someone who particularly likes kids. I think most kids drain energy away from you. I don't adore kids in general. But I really adore my kids. I think they're really, really interesting. And ever since

they were babies, I have pored over books like "Oh my God, now they're developing these small motor skills. And now they're following me across the room. And now there's been this change. And they're acting differently and why is that?" Intellectually, they were my little projects. And they were really, really interesting to me. And I've never felt that way about other kids.

Lily's case is representative of many of the women we interviewed: Work-life balance transforms over time, involving various permutations combining work and family—from not being employed for pay at all, to freelancing part-time from home, to now working part-time in a job for which she is overqualified but that allows her to check her work at the door at the end of the day. Children and "quality of life for the family" have been the driving forces in each of Lily's employment decisions. When Lily did eventually move back into a "regular" job, this transition was precipitated by financial concerns related to the children's expanding economic needs.

Lily's experience of being overtaken by unexpected emotions toward her children was a feeling we heard voiced often among women we interviewed. One woman summed this up quite succinctly: "I had no clue how much I would love being a parent and how intellectually, psychologically, emotionally and spiritually challenging it would prove to be." So while we want to be careful not to reduce the experience of motherhood to some set of gender-based natural impulses, and thereby ignore the diversity of how women mother, we also don't want to ignore the emotional or affective dimension of mothering.

Yet we recognize that when women say they like to "be with their children," it can come with qualifiers. And being with one's children can be a double-edged sword, captured by this mother's description: "I was surprised at the demands of raising children and equally surprised at how much I enjoyed being able to stay at home with my children." Another mom candidly revealed: "I didn't think I'd enjoy the time with baby games and I didn't. That's why we hired help." On the other hand, she enjoys and feels better equipped to do hands-on mothering now that her children are older. Therefore, while we don't wish to idealize motherhood as some gendered caricature, insider understandings of how the women we studied viewed the pull of children toward home are critical to understanding the intersection of gender, work, and identity in America today.

Parenthood, Mama Time, and Being a "Present" Mother

Many women want to be with their children. And, perhaps, many others do not. It is, however, a cultural norm that parents, and especially mothers, feel they *should* be with their children. Women respond to powerful societal norms that instill a particular gendered sense of responsibility for caring for their children. And, while "daddy time" is on the rise, for many women we studied that sense of parental responsibility is wrapped around spending time with their children.

While many men surely feel a sense of responsibility in terms of providing for their children and are acting on that sense of responsibility by spending increasingly more hours with their children, as we detail below, our research suggests that men and women may tend to act on this sense of responsibility differently. One woman described this in terms of the divergence in how she and her husband saw their responsibilities. She constantly felt pulled between work and the need to spend more time with her children, while her husband's self-described "duty is to continue to work until the children are eighteen." Men, therefore, may feel this sense of responsibility most acutely in terms of providing for their children *financially*.

For the women we interviewed, however, this support is often reckoned more prominently in terms of the *time* they devote to their children. Julie captured this phenomenon in the following story: Matt, Julie's husband, goes on a hunting trip with his brothers each fall. The year their daughter, Annie, turned thirteen, the hunting trip coincided with Annie's birthday. Matt forged ahead with planning the trip, expecting Annie could be mollified by a good present. Matt went hunting, and he bought Annie a cell phone. Julie couldn't understand Matt's decision to prioritize a hunting trip over their daughter's birthday. Yet Matt fell to stereotype and provided with his money, but not with his time.

A quick foray into the blogosphere will confirm that far fewer dads than moms spend time lamenting their lack of time with their children, being torn between job and home, and judging other parents based on how much time they spend with their kids. One article noted, "The ratio of trend stories about Mommy Wars to Daddy Wars runs about 1000 to 1, if you leave out stories about hockey dads brawling on the sidelines."[4] And even if men feel pulled between job and children, it's less socially acceptable for men to admit to, or to act on, these feelings. We view this not as a matter of inherited predisposition, but rather a feature of learned gender roles in our society. In the introduction to this book, we discussed how in our society the full weight of rearing children falls squarely on the shoulders of the nuclear family, especially before children enter school. One way of looking at this is that given this burden, dads and moms pay a different price.[5] Fathers feel pressure to support their children in terms of providing for them financially, while women feel they themselves should spend time with their children. Men are therefore conditioned to expect someone else will care for their children, usually their spouses.

Women who feel they should provide for their children in terms of both their time and their paychecks sometimes find that they need to give up the paycheck to provide the time. Talia, a medical doctor who opted to stay at home with her children when her husband changed career tracks to a much more demanding position, echoes this sentiment when she said, "I could have said my career comes first, but I didn't want to do that. What is most important is my responsibility for the kids." For Jennifer, the decision to stay home with her kids was based on a sense of moral responsibility. She described her decision in the following way: "If we were financially able, one of us needed to quit our jobs. What was the point of having kids if we weren't spending time with them? My children were being raised by strangers—sixty-five hours per week of child care. Deciding to quit my job and stay home with my children was *the right thing to do*." Therefore, even while Jennifer and her husband had entertained the notion that he or she could serve as caregiver, she was the one who quit her job. And, as detailed in chapter 2, among families where one parent stays home, ninety-seven times out of a hundred it is the woman who does so. This can be a decision based on the man's higher earnings, but the calculus by which families arrive at the decision about who stays home often cannot be captured by a spreadsheet and involves the social and cultural forces described earlier.

Many women who continue to work find ways to be more available to their children by downsizing or even changing careers. One woman told us, "I worked as a lawyer in a law firm and expected that I would be better able to leave the work stress at work. I wanted more vacation time and less stress so that I could be a more 'present' mother. I just changed my career from lawyer to employee relations in an urban school district." These women are describing their experience in terms of being a more "present" mother.

This sense of responsibility intersects in various ways with the expanding set of expectations of parenting in the twenty-first century. Marilyn, a sixty-five-year-old mother of six grown daughters, who qualified for medical school in her forties but was denied entry because she was told she was too old, observed, "Nowadays there are pressures that we didn't have to contend with: safety issues, scheduling play dates, hovering over children. We thought it was good for kids to develop their own sense of responsibility and self-discipline. We tried to structure routines with freedom."

And, as Marilyn aptly notes, parents spend more time with their children than ever before, and they certainly feel that parenthood has evolved into a more complicated job. In a 2005 national poll, for example, almost three-quarters of mothers surveyed believe that motherhood is more demanding now than it was for their own mothers.[6] For many women, there is a sense now that to be a "good" mother requires expertise in child development and increased time spent interacting with their children. Sociologist Sharon Hays refers to this as "the culture of intensive mothering."[7] Moms feel pressure to "be there" for their kids: arranging play dates, assuring educational play, providing opportunities to participate in lessons, and of course, driving them to myriad activities—year-round hockey camps for seven-year-olds and language classes for three-year-olds. And as the kids get older, the options expand exponentially. Societal pressures have dictated that "good" parents involve their children in a wide variety of activities.

Ironically, part of this need to schedule children, which complicates the lives of working parents enormously, has arisen out of women's increased employment. While parents used to be able to send their kids outside to play kick-the-can with the neighbors, now it's likely that the neighbor kids are in child care. If they want their children to play, they need to set up opportunities in advance. Also, more parents at work means fewer sets of eyes in the neighborhood to keep watch.

Despite spending greater numbers of hours at work, married mothers increased the time they spend with their children from forty-seven hours per week in 1975 to fifty-one hours per week in 2000. Working married mothers today spend less time with their children than at-home moms, but the difference in the actual interaction time is considerably smaller than you might think. While the differences in time spent on direct interaction with children is small (estimates range from one half-hour to one hour per day), the big differences come in the time nonemployed moms spend doing other things, like cooking or laundry, while the children are present.[8] Working mothers find time to spend with their kids by cutting back in other areas, sleeping a bit less and multitasking a lot more than nonemployed moms.

The baby boomers set the tone for young parents today. Overachievers themselves, boomers have carefully guided their children along the path to young adulthood. Cell phones, text messaging and instant-messaging allow parents to stay in close contact with their children when they're apart. Some parents have gone so far as to install GPS tracking systems in their children's cars and cell phones. Former Barnard College president Judith Shapiro wrote in a *New York Times* op-ed piece encouraging parents to separate from their college-aged children, "I have met with parents accompanying their daughters on campus visits who speak in 'third person invisible.'

The prospective student sits there—either silently or attempting to get a word in edgewise—while the parents speak about her as if she were elsewhere."[9] Yet, this is a two-way street, and while teenagers of an earlier era viewed college as a time to separate from their parents, today's college students are in quite regular contact with home. Undergraduates at Middlebury College in Vermont, for instance, were found to communicate with their parents on an average of 10.41 times per week.[10]

While we still argue that parenting is a gendered affair, modern dads are far more involved in parenting than their own fathers. Gone are the days of dads-to-be circling the waiting room until the nurse announces "it's a boy" or "it's a girl." Today's dads are there from the get-go. They change diapers, feed, and burp their children. They know never to say that they're "babysitting" their own children. Between 1975 and 2000, the hours married men spend with their children have shot up from twenty-one to thirty-three hours per week.[11] In short, dads today are actively involved in the lives of their children. But, while dads are doing more than they used to, they do not shoulder the load that mothers carry. We found that dads tend to be the one who is available for scheduled events such as sports and visits to the dentist. Moms tend to be the "Plan B" when things don't work out as intended. And, ironically, despite mothers' increases in face time with their children, they are the ones who continue to report not having enough time with their children.[12]

Child Care to Meet Comprehensive Needs

A part of the pull toward home revolves around a range of child care issues. Beyond wanting to spend time with their children, many women also had difficulty finding suitable care that met their family's needs. Aside from the availability and affordability of actual child care "slots," there are a whole host of other, less tangible issues that govern how and whether a family will outsource care. These issues contribute heavily to women leaving jobs and heading home.

Beyond the structural and access problems described in the preceding chapter, putting someone else in charge of caring for your child is a fraught issue for parents, especially mothers. A commonly voiced sentiment for women who do place their child in care is, "Oh, my daughter was fine, but I was a mess." As one financial analyst turned at-home mom described, it is often difficult to unravel the complexities of emotions and logistics when it comes to outsourcing child care: "It was a really hard time to hire nannies—the economy was booming. We hired some help but it didn't work out very well. We went through twelve possible nannies. When we did hire a nanny, [she] would get sick and we still had to cover. I also was really jealous of her, like 'Don't have too much fun.' 'Don't let him do anything new when I'm not there.' So I thought that was not a very good sign."

Another major hurdle families face is the quality, or perceived quality, of care available for hire. Some women simply feel that children fare best when raised by family: "The ultimate benefit [of my staying home] is the quality of the upbringing my children are receiving. They are being parented by a parent as opposed to spending sixty hours per week in a day care setting or with a nanny. This is the best of all scenarios I could have come up with for my two oldest." Another told us, "There's just a different benefit you can get when one of the parents is able to be there. The kids are different because I'm available."

Beyond feeling that only family can truly provide the highest-quality care, people have fears surrounding someone else caring for their child. Therefore, quality of care issues also intersect with the risk inherent in trusting someone else to care for your children. This risk can be seen in Jake's atypical but sobering story. The biotechnology specialist and his wife, married for six years, have two kids and one on the way. His wife, who stays home now, loved her former job as a nurse. They were happy with their home-based child care provider, who had a great reputation in their small town. Then, one night, county authorities called to say that their daughter's day care had been shut down. Their child care provider's sons had been molesting children in the neighborhood and in the day care. Jake said, "My daughter was an infant and never was out of sight of the woman who ran the day care, but . . . my wife quit her job immediately, and we haven't put our kids in child care since." Despite her readiness to give up working, Jake said his wife's job gave her a real sense of fulfillment that he doesn't think she completely gets from being at home with the kids.

Of course, this is an extreme example, and most children are *not* abused while in child care. Still it taps into parents' anxieties when leaving their children with others. Some families install nanny-cams so that they can keep an eye on things at home. Video recordings of nannies neglecting children appear on YouTube, and these videos garner considerable attention. Within a two-month span in early 2008, one such video had been viewed over 100,000 times.[13] Other families drop home unexpectedly to keep tabs on the nanny. Some feel that a child care center with multiple caregivers gives greater security, but, as noted earlier, spots in these centers are difficult to obtain.

The amount of child care needed by the family creates another issue, especially where both parents work in demanding careers. For the women we interviewed, this was a function of the sheer number of hours the children were in care, as well as the shifts required to cover the actual hours the parents worked, especially when work-required travel is factored in. It wasn't unusual to hear women report, as Jennifer did earlier, that their children were in child care upward of sixty-five hours per week. One Harvard MBA with three children whose husband had a very demanding job told us, "If I went back to work in any traditional position, we'd have to have two to three shifts of nannies and that's not an option for me. I prefer to raise my own kids." For many women, outsourcing child care took on extreme dimensions in the context of their and their husband's careers. And it was at that point that the women decided to scale back or drop out altogether.

Some families' care situations were compounded by their child's special needs. Special needs can be seen in kids with a medical or psychological diagnosis, but also in the case of "tweens" and adolescents who may require a particular kind of care that is difficult to outsource. Ann describes caring for a child with multiple medical and behavioral problems:

> I worked full-time as an investment management analyst in the USA until 1991. At that time, my husband and I returned to his native country so that he could take over the reins of the family business. Until the birth of our son in 1994, I did a variety of things in England ranging from teaching business English to doing whatever was needed at my father-in-law's company. For the first three years of our son's life, I was a full-time mother! Just as I was thinking about becoming active again in the family company, our son developed epileptic seizures. He was given the wrong antiepileptic medication, which resulted in ADHD, dyslexia, dyscalculia, CAPD, etc. For the past ten years I have been extensively involved in the myriad of therapies necessary for our son. I am very much a case manager for my son, and I actively coordinate and translate the information exchange that flows between our American experts and the doctors/teachers here.

Other mothers described similar situations: One single mother of an ADHD child noted, "He needed a lot of my time growing up. He is like trying to nail Jello to a tree." Another mother related, "[When] Everett was diagnosed with ADHD, I was the point person for managing his care and helping him succeed at school." A common thread in all of these cases is the responsibility the mother takes as "case manager" or point person—both duties that would be difficult to outsource to paid staff.

Some women emphasized the difficulty of caring for children not as toddlers, but as teenagers. One mom told us, "Conventional wisdom says we need to be there because we have infants. In hindsight, it's absolutely flipped. Now that the kids are getting older, it's more important for me to be there." A former bond trader noted that it was easier to hire someone to care for her children when they were "cute naughty" as toddlers, but now that they were not-so-cute misbehaving adolescents she felt the need to be more in charge of her kids' care. Echoing this sentiment, an assistant vice president of a foundation said, "When my son was about sixteen, I felt that it was important to be home during the unstructured after-school hours and went down to twenty-five hours per week until his senior year." Another mom said, "I find the teen years to require more parental time than toddlers and am glad I have the flexibility by having my own business."

In interview after interview, women told us how their decision about whether to remain working, to downsize, or to reorient their career revolved around children. Women routinely told us that a part of their decision whether to continue working after having children was informed by whether their income would cover the cost of child care. Rarely, as noted in the previous chapter, did women question whether working would cover part of the child care cost, presuming their partner's income would cover the rest.

Parenting, as we have argued, is a very gendered affair. And while we want to give voice to women's important feelings about wanting to be a great mother, we also want to point out how motherhood is also shaped by the society in which we live. Therefore, in this chapter, we have demonstrated how being a parent is conditioned by societal ideals. We have highlighted how the amount of time women spend with their children plays into ideal images of motherhood, and this can be seen in women's struggles over the competing pulls of work and home.

CHAPTER EIGHT

The Hectic Household

I'm late.
I'm late
For a very important date.
No time to say "Hello."
Goodbye.
I'm late, I'm late, I'm late.
THE RABBIT, WALT DISNEY'S
Alice in Wonderland, 1951

The rhythms of job demands vary. And in two-earner families, these two sets of demands increase exponentially. At the same time, children's needs shift from year to year, from month to month, from week to week, from day to day, and, as anyone who has made a trip to school to pick up a vomiting child shortly after dropping her off can testify, from hour to hour. The household, then, is the site where these fluid domains of children and work must coexist and compete for the scarce resource of time. And, women, as we have discussed, are most often positioned as the family's air traffic controller, managing this jumble of needs, desires, constraints, and opportunities.

This book aims to shift the unit of analysis for exploring the relationship between women and work from one where we look primarily at the women themselves to one where we take families as the point of departure. The conditions under which families operate have shifted significantly in the last generation. These shifts can be seen in the intensification in the scheduling of children's, and therefore parents', lives, and the concomitant increases in expected face time between parents, especially mothers, and children. Here, we look at how changes in parenting intersect with other shifts that affect family life to chart the emergence of what we call the "hectic household." Ultimately we consider how some women may feel pressured to respond by reducing, reorienting, or resigning their careers. It's useful to start with a bird's eye view into a day in the life of the hectic household.

Inside the Hectic Household

It's another Monday morning. Husband's on a business trip, babysitter's running late, and Amanda has a deposition scheduled for 9 a.m. Two kids need to be dropped off at two different schools, lunches packed, mittens located, science project transported. And Dad's not off the hook: Amanda will meet her husband briefly, when he flies in on Wednesday evening, at their daughter's piano recital to hand off the children before she heads to the airport for a twenty-four-hour business trip to Chicago, which will include a quick visit to her aging mother who lives there. And she knows that if anyone gets sick or flights are delayed this whole precarious plan dissolves, and she'll be scrambling yet again. Can this family keep it up?

In chapter 3, we presented a related scenario and explored how families who have followed societal cues to "do everything right" end up here: First was assiduous study as a high school student, which ushered in an enviable array of college admission letters. Weekends invested in the library yielded graduation with honors and admission to an elite graduate program, where, albeit cliché, she met her husband. The graduate program guaranteed entry into a fast-paced, demanding, well-paid job. Being mindful of the "body clock horror stories" she'd heard from friends, she gave birth to not one, but two beautiful children in her thirties. And, yes, she even got a boy and a girl. Successful husband, matched set of gorgeous children, fast-track job. She is the envy of women around her; she seems to have it all. Why, then, does every Monday morning make her feel like she's perched on the edge of some giant precipice? Why has she adopted the Nietzcheian notion "If it doesn't kill you it makes you stronger" as her personal mantra? And why does it feel mildly psychotic to have that as a personal mantra after all those years of hard work? What went wrong? And what does it mean for the rest of us, the students who didn't spend every weekend in the library, if even those at the top of the class are floundering?

This vignette summarizes the dilemma faced by many of the women we interviewed. While the previous chapters have examined competing claims about how gendered discrimination subtly works to push women with children out of the labor force or to limit their advancement, and how maternal heartstrings and the desire to do right by their children pull women home, in this chapter we revisit the concept of how *time* is an undeniably gendered variable in the women and work equation. And the limits of bending time is one of the most compelling reasons women voiced for choosing to leave their jobs or to reduce their hours at work to be home for their family.

These women were tired of the juggle, the struggle, the complex negotiations with their spouse over who, how, when, and where their children were going to be cared for, while simultaneously not dropping the ball at their own jobs. And even when they were able to square arrangements with their spouse, they were plagued with anxieties about the kind of care their children were getting by a person being paid to love their kids. These women liked spending time with their children and, certainly, the decision to leave their job revolved around having children. However, while many were surprised by the unanticipated pleasures of motherhood, few of the women described basing their decision on some primordial instinct to mother. Nor did they necessarily cease being ambitious in their own careers. They just weighed their options and decided they wanted to provide a saner, less hectic life for their children, for their partner, and for themselves. So, while walking away from a six-figure salary after years of study and hard work might seem irrational to some, it makes perfect sense when seen through the eyes of a mother who is in the throes of managing a hectic household.

Building the Hectic Household

While we have discussed some of the factors that feed the development of the hectic household, it is not something one buys into like a time-share or a new car. When women in the 1970s, 1980s, and 1990s responded to expanded educational opportunities, the implications of what they were taking on were not completely clear. They may have shadowed an attorney or a physician at the office or the clinic, but they didn't follow them home. Many of the women we interviewed described a situation in which they felt blindsided by the realities of a household juggling two jobs and a family. One mother describes her experience:

> Both I and my spouse have full-time jobs. Trying to balance two full-time jobs with the responsibilities of a family and a home has led to two periods of separation. . . . These separations and near-divorces cost money, time, and emotional and physical energy. If I had devoted more thought and reflection to balancing a career with having children *before* I was in the circus of it all, I could have saved our money, time, and energy. In the end, the loss of the money was not the important aspect since we both had good jobs; the real cost was in the emotional scar tissue.

Hectic households result from an additive process. We have demonstrated how shifts in societal demographics, such as increases in women's educational achievements and the later age at which women have children, set the stage for this evolution. Hectic households are built around having children in conjunction with the pressures imposed by dual-income families, and this intensifies when both parents have demanding jobs with seemingly insatiable appetites for a worker's time. Added to the encroachment of contemporary work culture on home life are the increases in expectations for employees to travel domestically and internationally, as well as to relocate.

And, somewhere at the margins of work demands is the overlapping load of the second shift, extending not only to the care of one's children but also to that of parents and other family members.

Having Children Changes Things

When Anne, who lives in New York City, had her first child, she and her husband began categorizing their social and professional worlds into what they called *wiks* and *woks*, those with kids and those without kids. They soon discovered, as many parents do, that having children changes everything. From your relationship with your partner or spouse to your relationships with your friends, everything shifts. No area goes unaffected, including work.

Anthropologist Arnold van Gennep introduced the idea that important and common rites of passage are connected with the biological stages of life—birth, maturity, reproduction, and death.[1] Rites of passage signal a renegotiation of relationships, as one moves from one status to another. Birth is a classic rite of passage for both mother and child. Accordingly, relationships are renegotiated—with one's spouse, with one's own parents, even with the state. Curiously, the only relationship that remains supposedly untouched is one's relationship with one's employer. And therein lies the rub for many women. While some women are able to "cut a deal" with their employer to accommodate their new status, they are often doing so on an ad hoc basis. Many women describe how they had to broker a deal with their employer to accommodate their new status as a mom, and some were hesitant to do this because they sought to avoid bias against them as a mother. We've introduced this topic in chapter 4 and will revisit it in chapter 12.

Many of the women we interviewed described periods of intense engagement with work before having children. "My husband and I would both be working late. Around 8 p.m. he or I would phone and say, 'I'm leaving really soon and I'll see you at home.' Forty-five minutes later one of us would call the other at the office and ask, 'You still there? Yeah, me too.' We'd laugh about it and agree to meet at home before it got too much later. It was kind of like a competition of sorts. We kind of reveled under the sheer weight of all that work. That *all* stopped when we had kids. Now if one of us stays longer at work than scheduled it means there would be no one to meet our five-year-old at the bus stop and our two-year-old's child care provider would start charging us a dollar for every minute we were late. Now when one of us works late, it's a major deal."

Other women echoed this theme of "putting in their time" before having kids to allow them more flexibility later in their careers: "I worked like a dog before we had kids and when my hubby was in grad school. Then I bought my own business and he got a teaching position—both before we had our first child. So we have a lot of flexibility in our lives now as parents and we 'did a lot of time' first in our careers to make this so." But, as we describe in chapter 4, putting in one's time doesn't work for everyone, and in many occupations, workers can feel like they are "only as good as their last sale," thereby upping the ante for what's expected of them on the job.

Therefore the foundation of the hectic household is children. It's not that dual-income households without children are not overworked and stressed. It's just that the addition of children significantly reduces a person's flexibility to respond to everything their job tosses at them. Some parents expressed fears that their own hectic schedule will cause their child to be stressed, and they sought to avoid this by altering their work situation.

The Twenty-First-Century Worker

We've also described the phenomenon whereby the combined weekly hours of husbands and wives, particularly among professional couples, are rising. In 1969, couples between the ages of twenty-five and fifty-four worked an average of fifty-six hours per week. By 2000, this had increased to sixty-seven hours. Average combined hours, therefore, have increased by almost 20 percent over the past three decades. This increase mostly reflects the steady rise in the number of working women, with those who work increasingly likely to be employed year-round.[2]

At this point in history, therefore, the demographics of who in the household works and how much represents a temporal threshold that feeds the hectic household phenomenon in particular ways. And this effect is intensified in dual-earner households where the challenge of meeting both sets of employer demands can be made even more difficult when priorities compete. One attorney turned at-home mom told us, "When our nanny got sick, my husband and I were always arguing about whose work was more important, challenging the other, 'When did you schedule that deposition!?'" Synchronizing calendars becomes critical to family survival, and a whole cottage industry of planning tools is being developed to facilitate this.[3] One Web site instructs moms on how to "adopt a mom-oriented calendar system, . . . identify overcommitment hot spots where rescheduling will be required to alleviate simultaneous events," and "assess individual schedules using family principles acknowledged by both Mom and partner alike."

The kinds of jobs parents hold also relate to the level of stress in the household. High-pressure jobs, particularly those with limited flexibility, are especially challenging for families. And, as we discussed in chapter 4, work-required travel has a huge impact on families. As companies have globalized, expectations for employees' travel obligations have surged. And travel is one of the most difficult variables for workers with children to manage. Lynn and Marshall, parents of a four-year-old, both work for the same convention hosting company. They both have to be out of town for work at the same time—often for a week or more. So far, they have managed to make it work by shopping for bargain airline tickets to fly one of the grandmothers to accompany them to the out-of-state conventions to assist with care (while simultaneously paying the child care center costs they have contracted for at home.) They don't yet have a plan for how they will manage when their daughter starts school and is therefore less mobile. The grandmothers are unable to care for their granddaughter for such an extended time on their own, and Lynn and Marshall neither want nor can afford to pay someone to care for their daughter round-the-clock for such a prolonged absence. Yet in the current economy they are hesitant for one of them to switch jobs. Travel, as we have noted, is one of the attributes of a job that may be attractive to a woman at the outset of her career, but a reason to quit her job after having children, thereby underscoring the notion that the building of a hectic household is an additive process.

And, even if women manage to cope with or avoid travel in their own jobs, they are often stymied by the travel demands of their spouse's job. Many women commented on how their husband's travel made it impossible for them to conceive of working full-time. Consider the case of Rita and her husband, Steve, both lawyers by training. Rita worked part-time from home and Steve worked full-time after their first baby was born. Dissatisfied with his job, after the arrival of baby number two, Steve took some time off and stayed home to care for their kids, while Rita accepted a full-time position. At the end of that year, pregnant with their third child, Rita committed to staying home full-time so that Steve could take a corporate job that required a good deal of travel and had a very unpredictable schedule.

> He could entertain taking this job, knowing that there would be a lot of travel. If I had a full-time job outside the home, I don't think he would take this job, because I think it would be too difficult. And that's based on knowing people in his line of work. Most people have spouses that stay home. Because when you have a spouse that travels a lot, it's really difficult. And we have known people who have a job similar to those and their spouse is working, and it's just crazy for them. It's really, really hard. And it's pretty impossible.

Rita and Steve made the joint decision for him to take this job, and they recognize that his job continues to determine the type of work (paid or volunteer) that Rita can do:

> The inflexibility of his job and the uncertainty of his hours make it really hard for me to even consider any kind of real job where I'm dedicating a certain amount of time, because of his schedule. I think that definitely has an impact on the choices I can make right now. And Steve and I will often say that, "Wow, I can't do that particular

job" because I can't count [on] that Steve will be home at whatever time, so that I can do whatever I need to do. But, his job, and the uncertainty of his hours, definitely limits the choices of what I do. And that includes volunteer work too. Where I can't count on that Steve's going to be home on certain days, I have to think about that when I take on something that is in the evenings. And so definitely it [his unpredictable work and travel schedule] has a huge impact.

Even working part-time can be difficult when a woman's husband travels. Leslie, a family therapist and mother of two preschoolers, cut her work time to two ten-hour days per week. Because she works "so little, that time is really precious." Therefore when "somebody is sick or something comes up," such as an unplanned business trip for her husband, their family really struggles.

And, if unexpected business travel is a pressure for families, job transfers are a huge blow. As we noted earlier, increases in job transfers are a distinctive feature of the twenty-first-century economy, with nearly 4 percent of the U.S. workforce moving each year.[4] In the words of one mother whose family had been uprooted several times, "Moving is hard as a mom. When you move to a new place, it's the mom's job to get the kids settled, figure out child care, get the house in order, and get your social network."

The Sandwich Generation

Supporting aging parents is a contributing factor in the hectic household, and a factor more families are likely to encounter given shifting demographic trends. We introduced this phenomenon in our discussion of the second shift. Families who think keeping two jobs and raising children is tough should try caring for Granddad at the same time. As the nation's baby boomers age, increasing pressures will be placed on boomers' children to care for their parents. "People who are eighty-five and older make up the nation's fastest growing age group, and 78 percent of these people live in their own homes or in relatives' homes."[5] And we can expect to see a sharp increase in the number of families caring for both their parents and their children simultaneously, as women are having children at older ages. The unexpected care needs of an aging parent can create a tipping point for many hectic households to decide that one parent should opt out. This can involve not only caring for your parents, but also negotiating this care with other relatives. Managing your parent's finances and other affairs, helping with maintaining their home, transportation, grocery shopping, and visits to the doctor are all necessary tasks that are difficult, if not impossible, to outsource. Betty's family is still reeling from the aftereffects of the negligent care her father received in a professional nursing home. He preferred to stay in a facility in his hometown, about three hours from where Betty lives with her husband and two children. With she and her husband working full-time and living so far away, Betty relied on the care facility to take care of her dad. It came to light that they were overmedicating him as a way of controlling him, which resulted in some additional health issues. With his health seriously deteriorated, Betty eventually moved him to a facility near her home so she could better manage his care and interactions with doctors. She was, as was the rest of the family, devastated by her father's experience, but caring for her children and her parent while holding down a full-time job was a lot for one person to shoulder.

Another struggle for women in this "sandwich" generation involves the pressure exerted on them to play a linchpin role in the family. Even if they are not physically caring for either set of parents yet, they still experience societal pressures to be the one who promotes family relations among the generations. Therefore, part of being a good parent means being a good child. We'll return to this topic shortly.

Dismantling the Hectic Household

If hectic households can be built, they can also be dismantled. In this section, we analyze the steps families take to confront the pressures created by the intersection of the intensive parenting demands, the increasingly insidious nature of jobs that seek to have 24/7 access to employees, the complexity of managing two demanding careers, and the strain of caring for aging parents. Specifically, we consider the actions of women who significantly reduce or resign from their jobs within this context, and how they perceive the benefits of doing so.

We have been making a case for why family life is entering a new era, and how these societal shifts play out in households. The specific conditions under which families attempt to function have shifted, leading people to adopt new adaptive strategies. Women are not going back to the 1950s, because the conditions of the 1950s no longer exist. Women are deploying new management tactics to cope with the exigencies of a thoroughly modern and uncharted way of life. In effect, they are devising strategies to resist the inexorable pull of the hectic household. While they may not be able to determine a law firm's part-time employment policy, they do have control over their own labor. Reducing or eliminating their work effort is, therefore, an adaptive strategy to manage stress.

For many of the women we interviewed, the decision to withdraw from the labor force was a process. There were some women whose careers ended abruptly when motherhood coincided with their role as the "silent partner in a corporate transfer." Another woman wryly remarked, "Having full-term, undiagnosed twins really threw a ringer into my employment plans!" For many more women, however, the dismantling of the hectic household was a gradual process, much like the process by which it was built.

One of the first steps women take is to begin the process of "thinking like a family unit." As Lily put it, "Life changed for me. And the world changed for me so much when I had kids—when I had to go from thinking of myself to thinking of myself as part of a family unit. It was very important to me that it functioned in the most healthful way." Some of the women made a conscious shift from "his and hers" to "ours," where the household became very fully an economic unit, with both husband and wife playing complementary roles. Liz explained the division of labor in her family: "That's kind of how we have it arranged is that I run the house and he runs his business."

Another woman describes the specific calculations she and her husband went through: "My husband is a pharmacist, a field with tremendous labor shortages. We are able to balance our work and family life with his "time and a half" pay from overtime shifts. He works around sixty hours per week and makes as much as when both of us were working forty apiece or eighty total—thus, saving us twenty hours per week at the same pay. He always says he could *never* do this if I was not taking care of everything else. This division of labor works very well for us. We realize that we are in a unique and extremely lucky situation."

In many cases, women described this as a harmonious process, with the women feeling like they had a good deal. (See more on this topic in chapter 11.) In other cases, women saw what they were doing more in terms of a sacrifice: "I have had to make numerous accommodations in my work . . . to help my husband in his career."

Closely related to "thinking like a family unit" was the theme of nostalgia. Nostalgia is a key factor pulling women home. Many women are responding to their own childhood experience—trying to meet or surpass their own positive experiences of childhood. Some had at-home mothers who were there for their kids with milk and cookies after school. On the other hand, others may feel the need to redress the rejection they felt as latchkey kids when parents were not there for them. As Lily told us, "It's really important for me to create a better family than I grew up in." Maureen echoed this sentiment, "I felt like I was going to die if I didn't get to raise my son. It was a really strong feeling. I have some abandonment issues from my own childhood and I really did not want to pass that on to the next generation."

While doing better by their kids was an important part of heading home, women also had mixed feelings about the overall impact of their decision on their children's notions of gender roles in society. Brenda said,

> Because I have three boys they need to understand that they have a strong role model of a woman in their life who has a career and who works and contributes to the family's income in some way. That's just really important to me. But at the same time it's not important to me that they somehow suffer for it. You know, I think it's OK for

them to see that there is an option for women or anyone to be able to do many things well.

Jaime, who currently is working, also spoke of what she saw as the importance of modeling gender roles:

> I think there's also a political piece to it as well for me. I think a lot about [this issue] for my daughter and for my sons. What's the image you have as a mom and a woman? . . . There's been tons of stuff written about women who are college educated who were highly successful in their jobs that quit to raise their family, and the message that that's sending to their children. I want my kids to see women working and being successful. And right now the nonprofit I work for, . . . its whole mission is inspiring girls to be smart, strong, and bold. And so I do struggle with that piece as well. If I'm not working and I'm just volunteering like lots of moms in our community, what does that say to my children about the value of women's work and what women can do? They really spend all their time volunteering in the classroom and organizing field trips and raising money for the schools and the dads go off and do their work and the moms spend their time doing stuff for school. So that is actually a factor when I think about having a job and what that's saying to my kids and what's the example that it sets in their future relationships and lives.

Another woman noted that she was very conscious of her reasons for leaving her job, feeling like she could leave her job with her head held high: "I felt like I'd had enough professional success that I actually consciously didn't want to have kids when my career was stalling, because I never wanted to feel like the kids were a consolation prize because I really couldn't cut it. I didn't want it in terms of them. I didn't want it in terms of modeling."

Benefits from Reducing or Eliminating Work

Regardless of the path by which they got there, most women we interviewed say they enjoy being at home, and that this surprised them. The biggest benefit was that of having more time and lower stress for their children, their partner, and themselves, citing "freedom" and "personal flexibility" as a benefit of staying at home.

Lower stress and more time for children were key benefits women described. Biological anthropologist Meredith Small, in summarizing the research on childhood and stress, describes the most recent research documenting the effects of stress in childhood well into adulthood, with some dire health consequences. And, she notes that "middle-class American kids can be just as stressed as kids living in rougher economic or social conditions. . . . Scheduled activities, lack of sleep, and complex family lifestyles often leave little downtime."[6]

We've focused on both the pleasurable aspects of being with children and how parents are logging more and more time with their kids, even if that time is spent in the car shuttling from activity to activity. In particular, we considered the expanding role of parents to *manage* their children's lives. Play dates, summer camps, music lessons, chess club, soccer, dental appointments, speech therapy, well-child checks—these are all aspects of modern childhood that demand a particular kind of parental intervention. Therefore, a big challenge women described was finding a way to mesh the time demands of work with the shifting needs of children over their life cycle, seasonally throughout the year, and with the addition of more children to the family. Flexibility was seen as an essential ingredient in blending job and family demands.

Women told us again and again how having the *flexibility* to be with their kids according to the kids' schedule was a big draw toward home. For reasons both symbolic and practical, women liked not having to split their time and attention between home and work. For Alana, it was a pleasure "to go to soccer games not wearing high heels." Angie told us, "I enjoy being able to pay attention to my kids when they need it. I'm not running at the frayed edge." Sue, a mother of two, noted, "I think that Sean gets a lot of mommy time, Sean and Ryan both get a lot of mommy time. And, I like to do things with them, like go to the zoo, and go to the children's museum. And Sean is able to take piano lessons, and gymnastics, and swimming. And this summer he did baseball, and soccer. Because I've got a flexible enough schedule I can just cart him wherever he needs to go."

Women also reflected on how their being home benefited their spouse. Creating more time for their spouse revolved around their role in helping their husband's career succeed by managing the household, picking up dry cleaning, planning the family's summer vacation, and so on. But it also was about the functioning of the "family unit," and about their relationship with their husband. One former advertising executive described it this way: "My husband says I run the back office. On weekends, we don't do errands, we play. I run a great back office." Other women report they do things to make their husband's lives easier and more streamlined, which in turn creates a better childhood for their children.

While we'll pick up this issue again in chapter 11, we want to note that the women we interviewed did not see their situation as a "he wins versus she wins" situation. Instead, women stressed that their families benefit from the way they and their husbands have negotiated the gender division of labor.

Reducing work time also creates additional space to spend time with extended family. Many women reported that one of the benefits of quitting their jobs was the increased time that they were then able to spend with their own parents. In some cases this involved expanding assistance to ailing parents, but in others it just meant increasing the amount of time grandchildren and grandparents, who are often separated geographically, spend together. Carol talked about driving across the country with her children to visit her mom for a month. Having the latitude to make this trip was especially meaningful to her when her mother died the following winter after a long battle with cancer. Sara, an at-home mom, described visits to grandparents in New Mexico and Florida. "When we go we stay for a week. Before I quit working at General Electric I would max out my vacation."

An additional factor to consider among women who downsize their careers or exit the labor force is that some can resume a sort of financial dependence on their parents. Being able to fall back on their parents creates a safety net for those women who quit their jobs. These arrangements can involve trusts and other financial support for grandchildren's education, thereby making up the resources lost when women opt to devote their time to raising their children rather than their career. Yet, as women noted, this is a double-edged sword and involves certain unspoken kinds of reciprocity. Women care for their parents and are often, literally and figuratively, the vehicle ensuring face time with grandchildren.

A benefit of being home that gets far less play than the pull of children or the push of the job are the gains women see in having lower stress and more time for themselves. Perhaps because women are supposed to be altruistic and put others first, we hear less about this aspect of the lives of women who reduce or resign their jobs. The opportunity to exercise is a benefit women who downsize or stop their career find. They also find time to relax, to explore creative outlets, and, once their children are old enough, to have downtime without anyone relying on them.

In some cases, women who have reduced their work hours to part-time or leave their jobs entirely do not express a desire to resume full-time employment: "I have always worked less than full-time. Usually two-thirds to three-fourths time. I think I imagined increasing hours as my children got older but it hasn't happened, and I still have two kids at home. Now I like the balance and may not increase when they leave because it is so nice!" Another said, "I don't consider that I 'chose a career,' rather I have sought out full-time, stable positions with good benefits to counterbalance my self-employed partner. I have also found that remaining underemployed contributes to a much healthier outlook (less stress) and a bit more time to contribute to volunteer efforts."

This chapter has described how women's exiting the labor force needs to be seen as more than just the push factors of work and the pull factors of home. The combined stresses of raising children while maintaining two demanding careers tax many families. A small number of women adapt to the stress by leaving their jobs. Many more respond by going part-time or forgoing advancement opportunities at work. And still others respond by absorbing enormous amounts of stress. And, yes, a few probably respond by feeding off the energy of dynamic work and home lives, but our research suggests that these women are a decided minority. Among those who do leave their jobs or otherwise reorient their lives in the face of family demands, the decisions these women make reflect something larger than individuals, their households, and their jobs. Their actions reflect a rejection in some ways of the frenetic pace that characterizes our society today.

CHAPTER NINE

The Professionalization of
At-Home Motherhood

I choose my choice!
Sex and the City, 1998

So what do you do? This question, which most of us might write off as "small talk," is anything but trivial. It reflects the importance we attribute to one's occupation as the primary source of our public social identity. So normally when we answer the what-do-you-do question, we identify ourselves by our occupation. We might say, "I am an attorney at Crawford, Ward & Neal," or, "I am a teacher."

Many of the at-home moms who left behind a career described the challenges of maintaining status in a society that dictates that so much of one's self-worth is created at work. Acknowledging their at-home mom status was something most of the women continued to grapple with or had struggled with in the past. This chapter delves into this topic of struggles with identity and describes some of the strategies these women developed to maintain their public social identity and private feelings of self-worth when they left their jobs, including how they frame their early exit from the labor force and how the changing demographics of at-home moms are professionalizing motherhood.

The Invisible Woman

Although most Americans don't like to admit there is a class system (we prefer to believe we accept people for "who they are"), we actually, and often without thinking, rank each other on the basis of our occupational identity. The women we interviewed point quickly to how Americans attach so much of their self-worth to their work. In the words of one, "If you're talking at a cocktail party you feel like a very boring person if your answer is, 'I'm at home with my kids.' Because in our society, most people tend to value—well, they define themselves by what they do. Even though I think raising children is very important and I wouldn't trade my choices, it's hard to hang your hat on that and define yourself in that way."

When some women left their jobs, they soon discovered that they became "invisible" in social settings. A former lobbyist noted that when she tells people she's now at home with her kids, the response feels to her like, "'I could have sworn there was a person there, but I guess not.' So you really are invisible to the rest of the world. You have to have a strong ego, and you have to be willing to have people turn and walk away because you're just a mom and, so, you're boring." Another mom echoed this sentiment when she said, "It's hard on my ego to be the stay-at-home mom. . . . It's painful to see people's eyes glaze over when I say what I do." Another said, "One of the biggest challenges of being a stay-at-home parent is you have to have a really strong ego, because you essentially drop off the face of the planet as far as the rest of the world is concerned. You don't exist."

But unlike H. G. Wells's character in the science fiction novella, *The Invisible Man*, who becomes mentally unstable when he cannot become visible again, the women we interviewed resisted society's attempts to recategorize them in some sort of diminished role when they left jobs for home.[1] In other words, they *categorized back*.[2] Here we look at the different ways women manage their identity in response to this societal tendency to marginalize them for their decision to stay home.

"Home, for Now" and Early Retirement

One of the key strategies women said they used to counter being relegated to the invisible focuses on the temporal aspect of their status.

That is, they emphasized being home as a transitory status, or as a new phase in their life after putting in their time at work.

Some women emphasized their at-home status as a temporary hiatus from the labor force: "It's so painful. I say 'I'm home right *now*.' I think I catch myself using that modifier a lot." Another said, "I am a doctor, but taking a sabbatical for now." Whether these women intended to return to work sometime soon, sometime later, or, possibly, never, by emphasizing the provisional status of being out of the workforce they were able to better manage the reactions of people who tended to dismiss them on the basis of their employment status.

Another way women framed their experience in terms of time was to use the language of "early retirement" to describe their employment status. Not unlike senior citizens, who also struggle with similar issues of social invisibility when they exit the labor force, these women described themselves as being a "retired attorney" or "retired financial manager."

In some cases, women felt that they had achieved a high enough level of professional success to merit retirement status. One way to look at this is that when they reached a certain professional standing, they "promoted themselves" out of the workforce and into a new at-home-mom chapter of their lives. One attorney reported that practicing in her profession for over ten years gave her "the right to claim retirement status." And, it was important to these women that they had achieved this measure of success before leaving the workforce. For others, they simply felt they had been employed for pay for enough years in their lifetime. And who's to say whether or not spending ten years working eighty-hour weeks is equivalent to a twenty-year career working forty hours per week? Kara, who had worked with the creative team in a home décor business since she graduated from college in her early twenties, simply felt like she had "put in her time" when her first baby arrived at age forty, and even more so when her second baby arrived at age forty-two, and was content to quit her job, raise her children, run the home, and provide backup for her attorney husband, who supported the family financially.

It is meaningful here to acknowledge that how these women describe their experience diverges from how others might "judge" what they are doing. A working woman in her late sixties, herself a mother and a pioneer in terms of her own educational achievement, responded to our study by echoing an argument made by authors such as Linda Hirschman and Leslie Bennetts, who have written about women leaving their careers to raise children.[3] She expressed dismay that women who had invested, and in whom society had invested, so much in terms of their educational training could take an extended break or even walk away from careers in medicine, law, or other specialized professions. What this observation misses, however, is the gendered double standard at work here: men who make their money and cash out of the labor market are seen to embody the ideal of the American dream—early retirement. What signals success like a suntan in February and a 9:00 a.m. tee time? Other men who are still working would, in turn, envy him. In contrast, women who invoke early retirement are seen as suspect—most stingingly, it seems, by women who are still working.

From Housewife to Homemaker to At-Home Mom

Since Americans determine value based on occupation, the professionalization of motherhood in the new millennium serves as a strategy for at-home moms to maintain status. One can trace the evolution through the labels assigned to, and created by, women who stay home with their children. Not so long ago, women commonly used the term "housewife" to describe their exclusive role raising children and maintaining the home. That term has lost favor among women. Jan recalled, with horror, when she unthinkingly wrote "housewife" as her occupation on a form for her class of 1982 high school reunion. "It's a 1950s thing, like I'm in my high heels with an apron making meat loaf. Which, you know, that's not what I do at all. It's a horrible title because it has such a horrible stigma to it. A 'homemaker' I can handle, but 'housewife'? That's like you're the servant, just a slave. You might as well just say you're a slave." She wished that she had written "stay-at-home mom" on the form instead. "Homemaker" was also a term some of the women we interviewed used and is an accurate description that captures the breadth of responsibilities these women undertake, but most described themselves as an at-home or a stay-at-home mom. Or, in some cases, women pointedly described themselves as a stay-at-home *parent*.

Staffing the Community and Maintaining Skills

Alternatively, if they remain outside the workplace for long, women may choose to maintain a sense of occupational worth by serving in quasi-professional roles, such as on the boards of civic associations, in positions with nonprofit organizations, and as aides at their children's schools.

Some of the women frame this service in altruistic terms. One woman told us that since leaving her law practice twelve years ago, she has worked twenty-five to thirty hours per week on "some very large boards, some start-up boards, some political organizations, some school-affiliated boards." She believes that she's in a privileged situation economically and this is a way to "give back to society." Another mom reported, "I have not returned to work in ten years. Frankly, I don't miss it. I also do volunteer work in the community to satisfy my need to feel that I am contributing to the world. I wouldn't change a thing!" Another woman spoke to how the various threads of self, service, and family reinforce one another in the work she does in the community and at home: "Because of family circumstances (spouse's earnings and values, choices regarding standard of living, etc.), I have had the opportunity to pursue lifelong interests and do significant work in my community while raising my children. Had I been employed full-time or part-time, I would not have had the flexibility I have needed to tend to my children's needs, nor the time to pursue my interests in community organizing and public policy."

Others view volunteer opportunities in a more utilitarian manner as a way to grow and prepare for future paid work: "Through extensive volunteer opportunities I was able to broaden and learn new abilities and skills." These skills can then be parlayed into bullet points on a future résumé. This is a topic we will revisit in chapter 12.

And, linking back in with our discussion of strategies to maintain an identity, many use intermittent project-based work to allow them to maintain an occupational title. One at-home mother of three demonstrated this strategy: when asked how she answers the what-do-you-do question, she said "finance and homemaker," before qualifying her response with, "I did do a little bit of consulting for random firms over the years." This example illuminates how the work-status categories of full-time and part-time fail to capture the complexity of women's lived experience.

Running with a Pack of Smart Women

In recent years, surprising numbers of women with professional degrees have exited the workforce. These growing numbers are reshaping the experience of at-home motherhood. As described by one former media consultant turned at-home mom, the at-home attorney, medical doctor, veterinarian, or business executive "runs with a pack of smart women." Another at-home mom of three with a Harvard MBA observed:

> At the preschool, there are ten mothers. I know them all pretty well. Three have their law degrees but aren't practicing. One was thinking about going back, and two weren't. Four have their MBAs, and none of them are working, outside the home I should say. One had a master's in urban planning and is thinking about going back two days a week. I look around, and everybody has an advanced degree. Two of the ten are working—they are the doctors—because they have to stay current. But even they knocked [work] down to three days a week.

Therefore, it seems to be increasingly easier for younger professional women to leave work or go part-time, as other like-minded women make the same choice. The result is the formation of social networks of mothers with similar backgrounds, which provide support, occasions for adult conversation that include but are not limited to domestic issues, and opportunities for their children to play together. What characterizes these networks are the similarities in the women's education levels and the professional lives they left behind. While it may be challenging for an ex-veterinarian to grapple with the loss of professional identity when she decides to stay home with her kids, this process of adjustment is made easier when her friends and neighbors are doing it, too.

Many women, therefore, reflected on the importance of maintaining connections with other moms with similar backgrounds, as a way of negotiating the process of heading home. One told us, "I also met a group of women at an ECFE [Early Childhood Family Education] class who were all largely professional women. . . . It's this fabulous network for highly educated women to find each other in the world of 'mommydom.' . . . I think it was a really big deal to have other professional women who I spent time with when the kids were little."

These social networks were an important part of the lives of at-home moms. And these women felt supported through their connections with women whom they saw as being like themselves: "It's easier to talk with people who come from a similar educational, sort of aspirational, background. A lot of that was, I think, having to do with the [subjects of the] conversations not being that stimulating themselves. It was good to have somebody to vent to who gets it—friends you can call in the middle of the night."

The importance of these social networks is not limited to the experience of women who have left high-powered careers. It was a theme in our interviews that cut across socioeconomic groupings, as seen in the words of one woman who left a midlevel management job to be home with her children: "I have a lot of really close stay-at-home mom friends that are able to do play dates and stuff. I think that especially in the summer, Seth would be totally bored if he wasn't able to get together with friends. So that helps, that helps a lot." Relying on social networks has always been a crucial livelihood strategy for families trying to get by on a limited income or weathering uncertain economic times. In some ways the reinvigoration of social networks among women signals a return to this way of life. A noteworthy difference, however, may be a heavier reliance on friends, given the reality that American families are now more geographically dispersed than ever before.

Beyond providing a social context for at-home moms and their kids, networks allow at-home moms to help one another out and engage in reciprocal relationships: "Yeah, we do trading in babysitting. If [my son] is over for a play date, then I can run to the post office." At-home moms excel at developing social networks that pay dividends in terms of sharing the care (and transporting) of children. This is contrasted with the experiences of working moms, one of whom told us, "I never want to ask anyone to help out when I'm in a jam with the kids, because I'm afraid they would ask me to reciprocate, which would be really hard with my schedule."

Another strategy some women use for enhancing social networks is choosing to live in a neighborhood where other moms stay home. Proximity facilitates these social linkages, and some at-home moms we interviewed were very connected to where they lived. "Especially in this neighborhood, there are so many people who stay at home. So it's good for Isaac to know that there are other people out there that he can go to if he needs them. And so, for him, it builds a stronger safety net, I think." While moms still spend a lot of time in cars, carting their kids around to visit friends, creating some sort of residential setting where kids and moms can "hang out" with other kids and other moms can be a way to forge social bonds that are helpful in meeting practical, social, and even emotional needs.

Women in recent years have discovered that with the spread of the at-home mom phenomenon, there emerged increased possibilities for the cohort of women you went to school with to now be at home. Mina, a forty-three-year-old mother of three and a former teacher who now works occasionally as a substitute teacher, said she is the only one of her high school social group of six women from Philadelphia who stays home full-time. The other five consist of two physicians, a biologist, a veterinarian, and a corporate executive—all of whom are pushing hard in their careers. Mina expressed that she always has felt like the one who didn't do "the career thing." In contrast, Sara, who is thirty-seven and grew up in Nebraska, noted, "There are seven women that I went to high school with who now live in the Twin Cities area, and they're all married and have kids. And, I'd say three-quarters stay at home with their kids—which is wonderful. Not all of them are home full-time; some of them are working part-time. It's great because we get together, and we've got such history that there's a safety net for me there, too. So, it's nice for Sean and Julie to have friends that they've known their whole lives, that they'll continue to know their whole lives." Therefore, while Mina's situation speaks to what it is like to be the only one who stays home, Sara's speaks to how this changes when a larger proportion of your group of friends from school also leave their jobs or shift to part-time work. While it is not possible to characterize women and their relationship to work by age alone, our overall research findings suggested that college-educated women Sara's age were more likely to be at home with their kids or reducing their number of hours at work than women Mina's age. We'll return to this discussion in chapter 14.

Taking the "Stay" out of At-Home Moms

At the outset of this project, someone rather unhelpfully suggested that we title this book, "Get off the Couch." While incendiary, this observation is useful for its ability to tap into a fairly widespread belief that at-home moms are somehow "working" less than the rest of us. This reflects a societal bias that values effort in exchange for pay over other kinds of contributions to a given household or the community at large.

We initiated our research by launching interview after interview with a question about how women spend an average day. While it was infeasible for us to "shadow" large numbers of women throughout the day, this approach allowed us to understand what women "do" with their time. We also collected time diaries from women, where we asked them to record all of their activities for a given day. We soon came to the conclusion that at-home moms don't stay home much. As one mother of three told us, "The only time I sit down during the day is when I'm in the minivan driving kids around."

In this section, we explore how being an at-home mom has little to do with domesticity, or at least not the homespun kind. It's about managing kids' schedules, carpooling, stretching the household budget, coordinating renovations on the house, waiting for the furnace guy (the phone guy, the plumber, the cable guy, the electrician, the exterminator), planning the family vacation, serving as a physical and social hub for the extended family, taking care of the pets, scheduling appointments for the family (doctors, dentists, orthodontists, optometrists, physical therapists, speech therapists, occupational therapists, teachers, principals, counselors, allergists), and shouldering the load of parental responsibility at school.

One of the key dynamics we observed was how much time mothers who were at home or who worked part-time spent in both public and private schools. We found that, ostensibly parents, but in reality mothers, were coordinating the arts program for their child's school, were working one-on-one as tutors for children who had difficulty reading, were teaching special class sessions, and were serving on committees charged with fund-raising and providing general support for the school. And all of this was in addition to the more expected roles of chaperoning field trips, supporting extracurricular activities, and helping with the school play. We did find dads involved in coordinating and supporting after-school sports.

In previous chapters on the changing demographics that have given rise to the 100-hour couple, the expanding demands of parenting, and how all of this feeds the hectic household, we've been building the case that in the absence of a job, women have very full and busy lives. Jill gives us an inside look into what "busy" translates into in an (albeit financially well-off) at-home mom's average day:

> I have a full-time nanny. I don't need as much time as I have, but I have her. She shows up at 7:00. I take Katy in carpool to school. I drop kids off by 8:00. Then I go to the grocery store. If I time it prop-

erly, I have twenty-three minutes. I pack things on ice so they can stay in the car. Then I go to a tennis lesson from 9:00 to 10:00 at a country club near the house. I go home, shower, get Harry to music class. In meantime, the nanny takes Sam to preschool. I pick up Harry and Sam. The sitter will have made lunch. Have lunch. I might run away and do e-mail or summer camp forms or pay bills or something. If I'm driving carpool, I leave at 2:15 to get kids. Some days one goes to swimming. The sitter leaves. I make dinner. We do homework, bath, and a video for twenty minutes. We do story time, and then bed around 7:30–8:00. It takes an hour to clean up after them. Paul gets home around 8:00, and then we sit down and have dinner together. We clean up and go to bed around 10:00 or 10:30.

In another household, Kim, a mother of three and former nonprofit administrator, describes how her day unfolds:

> I get up at 5:00 a.m., have coffee, and watch TV while I workout from 6:00 to 7:00 a.m. I get everyone up, feed them breakfast, and get them dressed. Ken takes the boys to school—drop-off is at 8:10—on his way to work. I drop Lucy at 8:45. We also have three dogs to tend to. While Lucy's at preschool, I try to run errands, which is hard because stores don't open until 10:00. I also volunteer at the kids' schools and prepare for Sunday school teaching, den mother activities, and some projects I am coordinating at the kids' schools. I pick up Lucy at 11:45, have lunch, tend to the dogs. Lucy gets some quiet time during this part of the day so I can "pick up" around the house for an hour or so. Then at 2:40 I head off to pick up the boys three times a week, when it's my turn to drive for carpool. We all get home, do homework first, and then the kids can play. We also fit in Boy Scout meetings, piano lessons, hockey practice, depending on the day. I also start making dinner. Ken works a lot of hours; many nights he doesn't come home until very late—sometimes till midnight. On nights he comes home, after dinner I'm done and leave clean up for them. The kids are in their rooms by 7:30. They can read in bed if they like. I'm in bed by 9:00. I cannot count on Ken to be

home in the evenings. He does make it home for hockey and baseball games, but he often has to go back to work afterward.

Clearly, there's not a lot of couch time involved in these at-home moms' days. While some at-home moms do lead a life where the full-time nanny can watch the children while Mom is at her tennis lesson, this is not the case for most at-home mothers. Many more moms are rising at 5 a.m. to get in some exercise before an obligation-packed day unfolds. Another characterization that is sometimes heaped on at-home moms is that their time is consumed by "frivolous" activities. Some describe the activities that keep at-home moms busy as "make-work activities." We're not in a position to adjudge how an individual spends her time as frivolous or worthwhile. However, many at-home moms who spend time planning a family vacation or overseeing kitchen renovations also make the informal infrastructure of their communities function. As one working mom we interviewed remarked, "Thank *god* for the at-home moms. They've saved me many a time when I've almost dropped the ball with the kids and school activities."

"I Choose My Choice!"

Among women, the phenomenon called "the mommy wars" pits at-home moms against employed moms, allegedly in battles over who does better by their kids, but, perhaps, more to the source of the issue, over women's decision to stay home and their reaction to other women who judge them for this choice. This cultural battleground is nicely encapsulated in an episode of the television show *Sex and the City*, in which Kristin Davis as Charlotte York indicates that she intends to leave her job in preparation for her upcoming marriage and future plans to have a child. When challenged by her career-minded, single New York City friends, Charlotte famously decries, "I choose my choice!"[4]

In this chapter, we've tried to give an overview of women who have "chosen their choice" and some of the struggles they encounter in maintaining their identity when they exit their jobs. In reflecting on the decisions of so many highly educated women to leave the workforce or to take themselves off the fast track to care for family, many argue that this harks back to the 1950s. Some, like author Leslie Bennetts, argue that women are making the "feminine mistake" by once again creating dependency upon their husbands.[5] The women today, though, differ from their mothers and grandmothers. Today's educated at-home mom is credentialed. While she may not be able to return to a position that pays as well as the one she left, she will still have labor market skills that are valued in the workplace.

And what is work? In societies like the United States, work is defined by payment or compensation for the worker. Broader understandings of "work" focus on the contribution of the individual to the household or the economy, and this is a topic we will take up in the next chapter. While many of the women we interviewed who had decided to stay home reported continuing to grapple with identity issues, very few seemed conflicted about their decision. Therefore, their conflicts stemmed mostly from how society evaluated their "choice."

Finally, it is difficult at this point for us to predict what these young professionals, now turned full-time mothers, will do in the future as their children grow up and they are once again free to work. The move home may only be one phase in a life of shifting pressures, opportunities, and associated identities. In the chapters to follow, we explore how women negotiate their at-home mom identity with their husbands and with their children. We will also consider other implications of heading home.

CHAPTER TEN

Financial Costs

I'm an excellent housekeeper.
Every time I get a divorce, I keep the house.
ZSA ZSA GABOR

This chapter analyzes the economic implications of a woman's deci-sion to take time out of the labor force. In addition to the obvious loss of income while out of work, women who drop out temporarily suffer a wage penalty upon return. For some couples, the husband earns more than enough to support the family comfortably, and the woman's income loss is easily offset by the gains in the family's well-being generated by mom being at home. This kind of calculation re-lies on her husband's continuing income stream. By leaving the work-force, these women take economic risks that at some point, whether because of divorce, disability, or death, their husbands will no longer support them and their children. Until now we have focused on the benefits accorded to families with a mom at home. Here we delve into the economic costs of that decision to leave work for home, and give some strategies for how families can manage these risks.

Take Time Off, Pay the Penalty

Leaving the workforce, even if only for a brief period, can have sub-stantial negative impacts on a woman's earning capacity. Women who have interrupted their careers for whatever reason return to work at salaries that lag behind those of their female counterparts who remained in the workforce continuously. A Center for Work-Life Policy study found that, overall, employed women who took time off suffered an 18 percent wage penalty. Women in business did better, with only a 9 percent loss, but women lawyers suffered a whopping 41 percent wage penalty for taking time out of the labor force. The wage penalties are severe, and the longer that women are away from their jobs, the more draconian the penalty. Across sectors, women who take a year or less off from work suffer only an 11 percent penalty, but if their break lasts for three or more years that number rises to 37 percent.[1] These penalties would be even more dramatic if they included lost retirement contributions.

Women who have taken time out of the labor force clearly take significant hits to their salaries upon returning to work. Unfortunately, these wage penalties seem to trail them through their working lives, albeit at a diminishing rate. To a certain extent, we would expect that holding all else equal, a woman who has worked continuously throughout her lifetime would earn more than a woman who had taken significant time out of the labor force.[2] What is problematic is that the penalties associated with time out of work are not commensurate with the length of the gap. One study found that even women who had returned to work twenty years ago still suffered a 5 to 7 percent wage penalty, as compared to women who had worked continuously, but with comparable levels of experience. This same study estimated that a seven-year gap costs women about ten years' worth of earnings.[3]

Despite the negative impact on their wages, many women we interviewed indicated that the decline in their earning capacity was easily offset by the gains from having more time with their families. Indeed, given that their husbands may earn enough to support them comfortably into retirement, the costs in terms of forgone income may be easily counterbalanced by the benefits they gain in terms of a less-stressful life. But what if for some reason, their husband's income disappears?

Does a College Degree Protect You from Divorce?

While many believe that divorce is a post-1960s phenomenon, the American divorce rate actually trended upward starting from the

Colonial period, only leveling off for the two decades following World War II. Beginning in the mid-1960s and continuing through the 1970s, though, divorce rates skyrocketed, more than doubling in fifteen years. After hitting a high point in the early 1980s, the divorce rate has roughly stabilized and even declined a bit.[4] While there is some debate among social scientists over whether the current divorce rate is closer to 40 or 50 percent, there is still a general consensus that roughly half of all American marriages will end in divorce. Yet when you break the rates out by education and income levels, the statistics tell a more nuanced story.

Up until the late twentieth century, college-educated women were less likely to marry than other women. This trend is now reversed—college-educated women are now actually marrying at a higher rate than less-educated women. A college diploma also seems to protect somewhat against divorce as well. College-educated women have consistently experienced lower divorce rates than less-educated women.[5] Even during the 1960s and 1970s, when college-educated women experienced rising divorce rates right along with all other women, they consistently divorced at between one quarter and one-third the rates of those without college degrees.[6]

Then, in 1980, something changed. The divorce rates for women without college degrees stabilized, with a roughly 35 percent chance of divorcing within the first ten years of marriage.[7] At the same time, the marriages of college-educated women appeared to strengthen. Over the past thirty years, the likelihood of divorce within the first ten years of marriage has declined dramatically for college graduates. If a college-educated woman married between 1975 and 1979, she would have had a 27 percent chance of divorcing by her tenth wedding anniversary. If she married between 1990 and 1994, her odds of divorce within ten years declined to 16 percent.

What do these ten-year odds mean for overall divorce rates? Demographers estimate that among failed marriages, 60 percent end within the first ten years of marriage. Extrapolating forward then, only a quarter of the college-educated women who married between 1990 and 1994 will divorce, as compared to more than half of those without a college diploma. Of course, these are only estimates that rely on assumptions of stable current divorce rates. Nevertheless, earning a bachelor's degree or higher gives a woman a better chance of marrying and staying married.

As we saw in chapter 4, higher educated women tend to marry men with similar levels of education. Their household incomes, therefore, tend to exceed those of households without college degrees. And, given that financial stress is a primary reason given for divorce, greater financial stability leads to greater marital stability. In fact, earning a household income above fifty-thousand dollars reduces the likelihood of divorce by 30 percent.[8]

Women who go to college are also more likely to marry later in life than high school graduates. People who marry later may have greater maturity with which to navigate the difficulties of marriage. They may have taken more time to choose a partner, and thus were able to make more compatible choices. Couples who marry at slightly older ages may have already passed through some of the stresses facing young adults, such as choosing a career or figuring out where to live. Of course, as we described in chapter 8, older couples have to navigate the stresses associated with the arrival of children just as their careers hit a high point in terms of time demands. Nevertheless, since age at marriage is such a reliable predictor of divorce, we would expect that college graduates would also have stronger marital stability.[9]

Whether or not a couple lives together before marriage also affects marital stability. Contrary to conventional wisdom, however, evidence suggests that couples who lived together before marrying are more likely to divorce than those who did not share a household prior to marriage.[10] College graduates are less likely to cohabit before marriage. Using data from the 1995 National Survey of Family Growth, Larry Bumpass and Hsien-Hen Lu estimate that 37 percent of female college graduates between the ages of nineteen and forty-four have ever cohabited, as compared to 46 percent of high school graduates and 59 percent of high school dropouts.[11] These lower rates of cohabitation may also contribute to their lower divorce rates. Whether the connection between cohabitation and eventual divorce continues is up for debate. Cohabitation has increased dramatically since 1960, and researchers estimate that roughly a quarter of all unmarried women between the ages of twenty-five and thirty-nine are currently cohabiting, while another quarter have cohabited at some point in their lives. Also, more than half of all first marriages are preceded by cohabitation.[12] As these trends do not show signs of abating, we may see significant increases in the percent of college graduates cohabiting.

Social attitudes towards divorce also seem to differ by education level. According to the General Social Survey, conducted by the National Opinion Research Center at the University of Chicago, women with college degrees have become progressively more conservative in their views toward divorce. In the 1970s, college-educated women were the most likely to think that divorce laws should be relaxed so as to make it easier to divorce at will. With each subsequent decade, however, women with college degrees became more likely to answer that the laws should be altered to make divorce more difficult, while high school graduates continue to be satisfied with the status quo.[13] Whether college graduates are leading a social movement or creating an even greater "divorce divide" by education remains to be seen.

While the outlook for the marriages of college-educated couples has certainly improved over the past few decades, the fact remains that one in four will end in divorce. And despite the gains in women's overall financial and legal standing over the past twenty years, women's realities in the event of divorce are surprisingly more negative than we had anticipated at the outset of our study. We had expected that women's gains in the labor market would have translated into a "softer landing" upon divorce. This is not necessarily true. While there is some disagreement over the actual number, many researchers argue that women's standard of living decreases by as much as one-third after divorce.[14] Single women with children are twice as likely to declare bankruptcy as married couples with children.[15] Men's living standards drop as well, but because they earn so much more than women, the drop is not nearly as dramatic as for their wives. Most divorced people eventually remarry, and remarriage is often the ticket for a woman's return to her former economic status. Divorced men are more likely to remarry and do so more quickly than divorced women. So for the 25 percent of college-educated women who do divorce, the penalty for opting out of the labor force to care for family may be steep indeed.

And, surprisingly for the women we studied, wealthy wives suffer the most dramatic declines in living standards.[16] In higher-income families, it is common for the husband to earn substantially more than the wife, especially if she takes any time off from work for children or to support her husband's career. Losing his income stream creates a precipitous economic dive for these women because they start from such a high level of household income prior to divorce. We are not saying that these women will enter poverty. It's just that they have further to fall relative to lower-income divorced women. They have the education and the skills to reenter the workforce, but, as described earlier, they will suffer a wage penalty.

Reality Check

Expecting to receive half of the assets, many women are surprised by the negative financial outcomes of their divorces. Methods of property division upon divorce vary by state. Only ten states employ community property laws, which treat most property acquired during the marriage, such as the family home, cars, or retirement funds, as jointly owned and to be divided equally in the case of divorce.[17] Any property that is brought to the marriage or inherited is typically exempt from community property. Of those ten, just three states require that assets be split fifty-fifty.[18] The others require the judge only to *start* with the presumption that the split should be even. The remaining states employ equitable distribution, where the court determines what is a fair and reasonable distribution of marital assets. Judges usually take into account factors such as the duration of the marriage, how much each earns, what each brought to the marriage, who took care of the children, and any accumulated debt, among other things. Usually stay-at-home spouses do better financially in community property states, while higher-income earners end up further ahead in equitable distribution states.

Women often are stunned to discover that they are not entitled to exactly half of the marital assets upon divorce. They can also be surprised that pension and retirement funds are not automatically divided; most states require a specific order to be filed in that regard. Alimony is another area where women are caught unaware. For example, one study shows that 80 percent of women assume that they would be able to receive alimony if they divorced, but in fact closer to 8 percent actually receive alimony.[19] Alimony—or spousal support, as it is now usually called—is not usually awarded in divorce cases, and when it is, the court typically sets time limits.

Beyond the impact on women, divorce takes a heavy economic toll on children. Children often have to move to less-affluent neighborhoods within three to five years of divorce.[20] Child support is typically awarded to the custodial parent, but collection of child support payments is uneven. A 2006 GFK Roper poll reports that only a quarter of the people who are supposed to receive child or spousal support receive the amount they are due, and another 30 percent are not receiving any of it.[21] While child support enforcement has risen dramatically in the past twenty years, the size of the awards is often insufficient to maintain the children's predivorce standard of living. Some of the increased protections for women come with a double-edge, though. Originally designed to keep the "deadbeat" dad from quitting his job to avoid having to pay child support, there is a rule that allows judges the discretion to impute parental wages. So if a woman quits her $100,000 per year job at a major CPA firm and then freelances to earn $25,000 per year, the husband can claim that the mother is "voluntarily underemployed" and ask the judge to use her potential wages in determining the child support awards. Thus, the support awards are conditional on the mother's potential income, not just her actual income.

The law doesn't take into account how difficult regaining their former wages is in practice for women who have left their careers to be at-home moms. According to the Uniform Marriage and Divorce Act, people are expected to "rehabilitate" quickly. In other words, spousal support is usually given for only short periods of time, in order to allow the at-home parent the chance to find a job, without recognition of the challenges associated with reentry. Judges increasingly weigh "helping" women become self-sufficient over supporting them as custodial parents.[22]

So What's a Girl to Do?

One way for a woman to protect herself in the case of divorce is to enter into a legal agreement, either prior to or after marriage. Such an agreement could specify how assets would be divided and what spousal support, if any, would be like in case of a divorce. Prenuptial agreements are typically honored by the courts, but rarely used. Since prenuptial agreements do not need to be recorded with the court until exercised, accurate counts of usage are difficult to ascertain. So while the actual number is up for debate, legal experts estimate that roughly 5 to 10 percent of couples write prenups before they wed.[23] Given the uncertainties in how courts will rule in divorces, we'd expect prenups to be used more often. So why don't more couples enter into prenuptial agreements?

First, couples may underestimate the chance of divorce. While the 50 percent divorce rate is a commonly bandied-about statistic, individuals tend to be far more optimistic about their own marriages. One study found that although they recognized that the national divorce rate hovers around half, the individuals surveyed perceived their own likelihood of divorce at just over 10 percent.[24] Another found the median response to questions regarding the chance of divorce to be 0 percent.[25]

Alternatively, an individual might hesitate to request a prenup for fear of sending a signal to his or her intended that he or she is less than fully committed to the upcoming marriage. In one study, almost two-thirds of the respondents reported they believe that asking for a prenup would imply uncertainty about the potential success of their upcoming marriage. Engaged couples may fear that sending such a signal might be detrimental enough to harm their relationships and perhaps even cause their fiancé to back out of the marriage.[26] Interestingly, in that same study, while only 16 percent indicated they would be willing to ask their partner to sign a pre-nup, over two-thirds said they would consider signing one if their partner asked.

But what if you're already married? Postnuptial agreements are an increasingly popular means for spouses to secure their financial position even after the wedding vows are spoken. While much less common than prenups, the usage of postnups, first appearing in the early 1980s, is on the rise.[27] In fact, 49 percent of the divorce lawyers recently polled by the American Academy of Matrimonial Lawyers report that they have seen an increase in requests for such agreements over the past five years.[28] Some marriage counselors recommend postnups as a way to relieve stress for couples arguing about money.[29] Recently, hedge funds and private equity firms have begun to request that their married executives draw up postnups in order to prevent spouses from making any claims on the funds. The *Financial Times* reports an extreme case in which one major U.S. hedge fund now refuses to take on new married partners until they have signed such a postnup.[30]

For our purposes, though, a postnup allows a woman who has left the workforce or otherwise downsized her career and earning potential to secure her financial position in the case of divorce. Such an agreement would set the value of her contributions in writing to ensure she is compensated appropriately if the marriage ends. Before leaving her lucrative law practice, Jennifer requested her husband sign a postnup:

> It was my decision [to quit], but I was very apprehensive about do-ing it for the financial reasons. I really didn't ever want to be in the situation where I was dependent on somebody else. And so I entered into a nonlegal agreement with my husband regarding our assets and regarding his future income, should we ever get divorced. I'm still contemplating putting that in a legal document, but I do have a writ-ten document signed by him, agreeing to what the financial situation would be. So I only agreed to stop working after I had an agreement from him, so he understood what that meant. . . . He said, "Oh, it's

ridiculous, we don't need to put this in writing." But I insisted, and we put it in writing, and he's agreed to give me half of his income for the rest of [his working life].

Jennifer would do well to consult a lawyer if she would like her agreement to hold up in court. Unlike prenuptial agreements, which are now routinely honored, the legitimacy of postnuptial agreements is still being tested by the courts. Historically, married men and women could not enter into legally binding contracts between themselves because the law considers a man and woman to become one legal entity at the time of marriage. Since spouses were considered a single person, they could not enter into contracts with one another. Additionally, the courts held that these agreements may be easily coerced within a marriage. Recently, however, courts have begun to recognize postnuptial agreements, although the enforceability still varies by state. Attorneys advise that to ensure enforceability, each spouse should hire his or her own attorney, both must fully disclose all assets and liabilities, and they must enter into the agreement without fraud or coercion.[31]

In the event of divorce, a woman's most reliable form of economic security for herself and her children, however, is reentering the labor force in a position commensurate in pay with her education and experience before she opted out, and herein lies the rub. Counter to what many believe, returning to the workforce is a lot more difficult than leaving it. We take up the difficulties associated with reentry in chapter 12.

Similar to divorce, disability and death are cataclysmic events that rock families. Even if women can count on their strong marriages, they don't always adequately prepare themselves for the possibility that their husbands may die or become disabled. Let's look at the more optimistic case—that is, when he is disabled. Disability is three to five times more likely to occur than premature death, yet most families do not insure enough to fully replace lost income. Typical employer-provided disability insurance plans replace up to 60 percent of income, but usually also set monthly maximums between five thousand and ten thousand dollars. For high-earning workers, these caps could easily force replacement income well below 60 percent.[32] Perhaps this is why one of our husbands remarked (jokingly, we hope) that if we run him over with the car, we should be sure to back up and finish the job!

And what happens to women when their husbands die? During the 1990s, roughly 13 percent of widows suffered income declines of more than half in the first year after their husband's death. Surprisingly, well-off women are the most vulnerable to those reductions, perhaps because, relative to their lower-income sisters, they are more likely to make considerably less money than their husbands.

Life insurance can moderate declines in living standards for wives who either don't work or who are secondary workers. Yet, not surprisingly, most Americans are "underinsured." At the risk of sounding as if we're getting a kickback from the insurance industry, most Americans do not insure adequately at critical life stages, such as when they are young with children. In fact, one study finds that close to two-thirds of secondary earners between the ages of twenty-two and thirty-nine would have projected reductions of living standards in excess of 20 percent, and almost one-third would face reductions in excess of 40 percent. Suppose we define a household to be "at-risk" if there would be a significant decline in living standards upon the death of a spouse. Under such a definition, for ages twenty-two to thirty-nine, only 20 percent of those at-risk households held sufficient life insurance policies to offset serious financial consequences.[33]

How Much Is Enough?

So, where does this all take us? Many women, when faced with these issues, want to know "how much is enough." In the case of widowhood or disability, if a woman wants to replace her husband's income completely, a rule of thumb is to insure for an amount roughly ten times his annual income. If she invested that money and earned a return of 8 percent, she would be able to fully replace his income for twenty years. Alternatively, she could perpetually replace 80 percent of his income under such a scenario.

In reflecting on the decisions of so many highly educated women to leave work for home, many hark back to the 1950s, claiming that, like most of history, the move to the hearth evidenced in the middle of the twentieth century is repeating itself. Some, like author Leslie Bennetts, argue that women are making the "feminine mistake" by once again creating dependency upon their husbands.[34] The women today, though, are not like their mothers and grandmothers. Today's educated at-home mom has options. While she may not be able to return to a position that pays as well as the one she left, she will still have labor market skills that are valued in the workplace.

In this chapter we have explored the economic implications of a woman's decision to drop out of the workforce. When women give up their paychecks, they expose themselves not only to the economic risks we outlined in this chapter, but also to a potential change in the power dynamics in their households. In the next chapter, we continue to explore the financial implications of leaving the workforce by examining how, after quitting work, women renegotiate their power relationships with their husbands, their children, and even their community.

CHAPTER ELEVEN

Negotiating without a Paycheck

The Golden Rule:
He who owns the gold,
makes the rules.

OLD ADAGE

Money is power. And when women give up their paychecks, the power balance in their relationships necessarily changes. This chapter explores how women navigate the potential and real changes in their power relationships with their spouses after leaving the workforce. Recognizing that a new at-home status can affect many different relationships, this chapter also analyzes how women renegotiate their relationships with their children, their siblings, their parents, and even their community.

Bargaining power is anything that allows a person to have influence over a decision. In the context of a marriage, we think of bargaining power as being a measure of the influence over household decisions that one spouse has relative to the other. Some people are uneasy with using the term with respect to married couples, thinking that bargaining belongs in labor disputes, not in marriages. Conjuring up images of winners and losers, this view of bargaining does not fit well with the notion that married couples love each other and share common interests. We don't like to think of ourselves as trying to get a bigger share, and thus leaving our partner with less. Yet bargaining does not have to be a zero-sum game in which one person's loss equals the other's gain. Bargaining may in fact lead to an outcome where both partners benefit.[1]

Couples bargain over decisions all the time, and that's because while they share common interests, they also hold individual desires. It's easy to imagine how competing individual desires lead to negotiation. It's Saturday morning, and she wants to work out while he wants to golf, but someone has to be home with the baby. This couple will negotiate to meet their individual desires. Maybe he'll get to golf this weekend, but she can look forward to exercising plus a lunch out the following Saturday. The negotiation to meet individual needs is fairly obvious, but even common desires can necessitate negotiation. A couple may each want what's best for the family, but at the same time they may have different opinions on which outcome is best. They may both want their kids to be physically active, for example. He wants them to play hockey, but she's worried they'll get hurt, so she prefers soccer. Even common interests may yield negotiable outcomes. In some cases, the couples themselves don't realize they are negotiating. One of the women told us, "I don't know who it was who said every time you make a major change in life you have to renegotiate the contract. And I never realized that that's what we were doing. But in a sense that's what we've done, with every big change we've sat down and had multiple discussions, not just one, about how you see the role changing, and what can each of us do to help the other person."

Sometimes the decisions are major. What school should we send the kids to? What house should we buy? What city should we live in? These types of decisions are typically decided over long periods of time. Other times the decisions may be more mundane and have to be made on a daily basis. Who will take the dog to the vet? Who will stay home to let the plumber in? Sometimes the bargaining is explicit, where the couple discusses the options and makes a decision. As we discussed in chapter 10, some couples go so far as to put some of their negotiated agreements in writing, such as in pre- or postnuptial agreements. Other times, the bargaining may be implicit. It may be that one spouse always does the grocery shopping, and that decision, once made, is not renegotiated each week.[2]

Many women related that they negotiated their roles very early in their relationships. One formerly divorced, and now remarried, mom described how the lessons she learned in her first marriage led her to be more purposeful in negotiating with her second husband. "My husband and I negotiated our marriage plans and family expectations and individual responsibilities for two years before we were married. We had every discussion I had failed to have in my first marriage. We have had an equal partnership that works for us for the past twenty-five years." Some had less positive experiences: "I agreed early in my marriage that of the two careers, mine was the more 'flexible.' Three times I changed states and jobs due to my spouse's career opportunities. It was hard and I am tired of starting over. This issue contributed to, but did not cause, our divorce."

Threat Points: Measuring Bargaining Power

Measuring bargaining power is not an easy task. Economists measure bargaining power by the best alternative an individual has to the outcome proposed by the other, and the better your alternative, the more bargaining power you hold.[3] A hypothetical example illustrates the concept. Consider a couple who have lived together for twenty years in a traditional marriage. The husband has worked full-time, while she has raised the children and managed the home. Since she has not developed marketable skills during these years, it is unlikely that she could secure a high-paying job. Her best alternative to the marriage is a living standard far below the one she is used to. His best alternative would not lower his living standards measurably, as his income stream will continue even after divorce and he could hire someone to manage his home. Understanding these alternatives, the wife may be willing to concede in arguments in order to remain in the marriage. She may yield more quickly and he may persevere in his opinions longer because they both realize that she needs the marriage more than he does. The point at which she would be better off leaving the marriage than remaining under the conditions imposed by her husband can be called a "threat point."[4] Her decision to care for family and home in the place of paid market work lowered her threat point substantially.

Having an income certainly raises a woman's threat point, as women's options outside of marriage improve if they have money of their own. Having children may lower the threat point of the mother, but also of the father. It's one thing to leave your husband and accept a lower standard of living, but it's quite another to subject your children to those circumstances. At the same time, mothers often gain custody of minor children, and fathers may worry that their relationships with the children might deteriorate upon a divorce. Thus, the notion of "staying together for the children" can be framed as a decision forced by changing threat points.

Economic theory implies that income provides bargaining power because it improves the best alternative for the one earning the money. Thus economics predicts that when they leave the labor force, women's bargaining position should change vis-à-vis their spouses. These notions may seem cold and calculated. Surely, for the most part, married couples love and respect each other. Her husband wants her to be happy for her own sake, because he loves her—he doesn't only strive to make her happy because he knows she can walk out on him. And that love for her increases her bargaining position. Recognizing he'd be devastated without her, he thinks twice about the demands he makes on her. In this case, the wife has something other than income to increase her bargaining position.

Most of the women we interviewed reported feeling a fairly equal balance of power in their relationships. Clearly these women have other bargaining chips that allow them to maintain power in their relationships. When asked about this, many reported that their husbands truly appreciated the benefits they gained by having their wives be more available at home.

For some, having their wives at home helps them feel better about the impact of their own travel requirements on their children. Take Peter and Sophia, for instance. Peter works in private equity and often has to travel away from home. Sophia is a former executive with a major media company. Now home with three children, she believes that her husband appreciates her being there because he is away so much: "He has said, 'I'm just so glad that you're here with the kids because I feel terrible that I've got such demands and I can't be around. It makes me feel better to know that they're [with you].'"

Several women commented that their husbands appreciated being able to focus on family and have down time with their wife and kids when they got home from work. They see their husband's and their contributions in terms of teamwork. Pam, a former bond trader, reported that her being home has made her husband's life easier: "He enjoys his children more because he's not worrying about the day-to-day. He is able to spend more time with the kids, coaching sports, etc."

These women describe happy marriages. They and their husbands do not perceive any threat of divorce. Still, a threat exists. These women are highly educated, and with their credentials they could easily return to work. One woman, who has an MBA from Harvard Business School, reflected on the importance of that credential to her ability to stay at home with their children:

> I love having the education and the experience that I have and knowing that I can take care of myself if I had to, if anything ever happened. One thing that I love about this MBA degree is that there's a huge network of alums and friends I have that I could tap if I had to find something to do to take care of myself. And I think if I didn't have that security that I have there, knowing that that's something I could tap, then I know I would also be out there working, to keep that there.

This threat that, if unhappy at home, she might get a job and destroy the comfortable support system he has come to rely on, serves to mitigate the increased power her husband might otherwise enjoy.

Negotiating without a Paycheck

Nevertheless, even though they are satisfied with their marriages and don't want to trade places with their husbands, when probed some women described how their relationships changed after they left work. Some reported that when their husband became the sole income earner, his work time expanded as his home effort simultaneously decreased dramatically. They reported that they miss being more of an equal partner in the activities at home: "I liked when my husband shared responsibilities." In some of these cases, women reported that their husbands play the "I'm the one who goes to work every day" card when they want to avoid contributing to household tasks. They argue about who's responsible for the children in the evenings, with wives saying they've been with the kids all day and their husbands responding, "Well that's your job." These women feel abused by this sentiment. Their husbands don't work twenty-four hours every day, seven days per week, so why should they?

Some women lamented the loss of what they call "fuck you" or F.U. money. This term, usually used in reference to amassing enough wealth to be able to tell your boss where to go when you want to quit your job, has been adopted by women describing financial independence from their husbands.[5] For some women who had given up working, the movement away from financial independence was challenging:

> I still wish I could earn my own money. . . . I have a friend who calls it "fuck you money." She loves her husband and everything. But people have all kinds of weird financial situations. Let's say you're a terrible shopper and you love to shop. And you waste all kinds of money and your husband's always auditing you and you fight about it every week. If you have your own fuck you money, you can do that and he won't audit you and it was your choice and that's OK.

In a twist on this idea, a 2007 New York Times article reported that the number of women paying in cash for luxury personal goods has increased in the last several years. The article implied that women are paying in cash to disguise these purchases from their husbands. Some women hope to avoid an argument with a husband. Others "say they simply feel a sense of freedom from pulling the wool over their husbands' eyes."[6] Strategies like withdrawing small amounts of money from an ATM and hoarding it, writing checks for an amount over the purchase price, or inflating the cost of certain items and skimming off the top when the husband forks over the cash all seem to "harken back to a time when far fewer women worked and in some cases received allowances from their husbands, whose hold on the family purse strings enforced their power as head of household."[7]

Perceptions of bargaining power also may differ from reality. A 2005 Harris Interactive Survey of wealthy couples found that two-thirds of the wives believe they jointly make financial decisions with their husbands. Yet when the husbands are surveyed, more than half view themselves as the primary financial decision maker.[8] A 2007 survey found similar results. Almost 60 percent of affluent men report that they make the financial decisions, while an equivalent number of affluent women claim that financial decision making is a joint effort.[9] This raises the question as to whether the decisions are really joint, with the husbands only perceiving they are making the final decisions. Or do the men make the decisions while letting their wives believe that their opinion matters jointly? In any case, a disconnect between who makes the decisions and who believes they are making decisions exists for a large number of affluent couples.

Women also are more likely to report that income does not drive influence over nonfinancial decisions. The 2005 Harris Interactive survey found that more than half of the affluent men surveyed believe that the partner with the higher income has a greater say in nonfinancial decisions. More than two-thirds of their wives, however, believe that the higher earner does not have a larger influence over nonfinancial household decisions.

Despite these differences in perceptions, both husbands and wives believe that when push comes to shove, the husbands will make the final decision. A 2006 *Money* magazine survey found that when couples disagree about money, the husband's opinion usually wins out, and interestingly enough, this was true especially in higher-income households.[10]

That same survey discovered that husbands and wives tend to divide up finance-related tasks in traditionally gendered ways. Men are more likely to handle the long-term investments and planning: almost three-fourths of those surveyed reported that men were primarily responsible for investment decisions, two-thirds for retirement planning, and almost two-thirds for buying insurance. The women are more likely to take charge of managing the household's daily finances. In nearly two-thirds of the couples, the women took primary responsibility for day-to-day spending, and well over half pay the bills and do the household budgeting. And these results match the experiences of our sample of women. As we noted in chapter 5, women were more likely to report doing the majority of the bill paying, while their husbands were more likely to manage investments. As the *Money* article states, "The gender divide seems to conform to some of our hardest-to-shake stereotypes. Man hunt food; woman make cave pretty."[11]

Bargaining with the Kids and the Community

To this point, we have focused on a woman's relationship with her husband. But the decision to leave the workforce also shifts the relationship between the woman and her children, the woman and her extended family, and the woman and the community. In effect, she has to carefully manage these relationships, in addition to that with her spouse, or she risks being taken for granted by all of these constituencies. Some of the women we interviewed were concerned about how their children viewed them as an at-home mom. These women talked about wanting to model a more equal relationship for their children. One woman reflected on why she wanted to engage at least part-time in the paid labor force: "I want them to know that I am working, that I am engaged, that I am a whole person, that I'm not there to serve them pizza when their friends walk in the door constantly and to pick up their laundry behind them as they throw it on the floor or take the cereal bowl to the sink."

The decision to reduce their workload affects women's bargaining power in other family relationships as well. As we discussed in chapter 5, women are often called upon to care for aging parents. We already know that daughters provide, on average, more time doing elder care than sons. Piling on a stay-at-home status further increases those expectations, both on the part of her parents and her employed siblings. Just as husbands sometimes claim work status (his as employed, hers as caretaker of all things at home), siblings can also put pressure on women who are at home or working on a reduced schedule to pick up the slack in caring for parents. One self-employed woman commented that her family expected her to handle her mother's health care, including spending many hours at the doctor's office, because she was the sibling with the flexible schedule. "What they don't seem to understand is that if I don't work, I don't get paid. At least they can get paid time off."

Even a woman's bargaining position relative to her community changes. If you have a child in elementary school, you know that many of the people who carry the load of volunteer work are at-home moms. While they may enjoy the work and most are happy to do it, some at-home mothers feel overwhelmed by the expectations and requests for their time. It is easier to say no to yet another committee if you have a full-time job. One mother, after spending a year when she was working what came close to full-time hours on her volunteer duties in addition to caring for her school-aged daughter, decided to take what she termed "a domestic sabbatical." She felt that she needed to take a stand to hold firm against the on-slaught of requests for her time. By invoking a domestic sabbatical, she made the presumption that she'd accept a task move from "yes" to "no." This strategy helped her move off the community's A-list of volunteers.

Bargaining power is difficult to measure, but usually fairly easy to feel. Women who give up or reduce their incomes open themselves to a potential change in the power dynamics with their spouses. They also expose themselves to being taken for granted by their children and the communities that rely on their unpaid labor. Yet, most of the women we talked with reported a continued balance of power in their relationships. Educated women today seem to have an easier time maintaining their status vis-à-vis their husbands, per-haps because despite leaving the workforce, they retain a capacity to earn that garners them leverage at home.

In this and the prior chapter, we examined the financial implications of leaving work, in terms of reduced earning potential, risk of lost or reduced spousal support, and potential changes in power dynamics. In the next chapter, we turn our attention away from the decision to leave work and its aftermath and explore what happens if a woman wants to go back to work after some time away.

CHAPTER TWELVE

Reigniting the Career

It's not where you came from,
it's where you're going that counts.

ELLA FITZGERALD

A woman who wants to reignite her career will confront many challenges, whether she has been out of the workforce for some time or has placed her job in a kind of holding pattern for family reasons. The transition will undoubtedly be complicated by factors both within her control, such as the type of job she applies for or type of retraining she might acquire, and also outside her control, such as how employers will view her hiatus. In this chapter, we turn our attention to these challenges and the opportunities women face when they are ready to opt back into or to jumpstart their careers.

While the first and second stages of developing a career and then scaling it back have been the focus of much of this book, this chapter analyzes the third stage. What happens as these women begin to move back into paid employment or ramp up their careers? What kinds of jobs do they want? What kinds of jobs do they get? How hard will it be to reenter the world of work? What strategies and resources might help them accomplish their goals? And how do changing economic times shape all of this? In this chapter we explore the myriad issues surrounding this challenging process of reigniting one's career.

A striking finding of our research is that most of the women we interviewed who left fast-track jobs did not express a desire to return to that kind of a position. When these women return to the paid labor force, they want to do interesting and meaningful work, but not necessarily in the field they had worked in prior to leaving their jobs. One way to interpret this reorienting of their career aspirations is that these women had been pushed off the fast track into second-tier jobs.[1] This is likely the case for some women. Another way to interpret this, and the women we interviewed tended to employ this characterization, is that they are starting a new chapter in their lives. In an earlier chapter, they were financial managers. Now, they want to retrain to become social workers for the elderly. This way of seeing women's relationship with work is consistent with the idea that women tended to see their lives, their work, their children as a sort of "spiral," rather than as a linear upward progression. We explore these ideas further in this chapter.

Before we delve into the details about the process of reentering or ramping back up in the world of work, however, we want to emphasize that not all women want or feel they need to do so. In this book, we have explored many of the reasons women might have for deciding against a return to work or a resumption of a high-intensity career, including ongoing care demands of their own and their extended family, pressures imposed by their husband's job, lack of financial necessity to do so, and that they may simply enjoy their life without a job.

One dimension that we haven't yet broached, however, is how the trend of working women delaying childbirth shapes women's decisions regarding reentering the workforce. Women today are older when they have children. The average age that a woman gives birth to her first child has risen from 21.4 in 1970 to 25.2 years in 2005.[2] But not only are women older when they have their first child, increasing numbers of women are still having children well into their forties. Women we interviewed who had delayed having children and who left their job after the birth of their child referred to their change in employment status as "early retirement." Suppose a woman has a child at age forty-two; if she were to reenter the labor force when the child heads off to college, she would be doing so at age sixty. While there is nothing wrong with going back to work at sixty, this was not in the plans of many of the women we interviewed. Much of the literature on reentry considers women who had their children earlier in life. And, having a baby at age twenty-four and returning to work when the child is grown is quite different from having a child at age forty-four.

Reentry Realities

Many of the so-called opt-out women we interviewed indicated they would like to return to the paid workforce at some point in the future. These women expect that as their children get older, they will transition back into the labor force. "Older" means different things to different people, though. For some, this meant when their children begin school, for others when their children are in middle school, and for others when their children head off to college. And, for those women whose children span a wide range of ages, plans to reenter can be contingent on all of these issues.

Reentering can be challenging, however. Employers question résumé gaps. Rapid technology change may have rendered skills obsolete. Changing economic circumstances affect the availability of jobs. A Work-Life Center survey of highly qualified women found that only about three-quarters of the women who wanted to return to the workforce were able to secure employment, and this was in 2004 when the U.S. economy was growing strong at a rate of about 3.6 percent.[3] Notably, only 40 percent returned to full-time paid work. Almost a quarter returned in a part-time capacity and about 10 percent became self-employed.[4] And, according to a 2005 study by the Forte Foundation and the Wharton Center for Leadership and Change, half of the highly educated women who had "stepped out" from work to raise a family reported feeling discouraged by employers regarding opportunities to return to full-time employment. These women reported being unprepared for the obstacles they faced upon reentry, and most did not return to positions similar to the ones they had left. Of the respondents who returned to work, almost two-thirds changed industries, and almost half became self-employed.[5]

However, as we noted earlier, it may be too limited a perspective to see these changes in women's careers as entirely negative.

Most of the women we interviewed said that while they envisioned returning to work, they did not want to return to their former positions, or even their former fields. Many of them described how they had achieved professional success in their careers before they left them, so, in effect, they had nothing to prove by going back to their former jobs. These successful women bring a level of confidence to discussions about future work. A former financial analyst reported: "I've always felt that when I wanted to go back to work, I would do an OK job of getting hired. I've rarely had the same job twice and I feel pretty confident in my ability to eventually talk myself into a job I'll like. So that hasn't bugged me particularly. I don't think I would be at the same level that I was getting paid before, but I don't need to be at the same level. I could move down a number of notches and still be perfectly happy." Given that the average woman holds ten jobs between the ages of eighteen and forty, these women look at their time at home as just another phase in their lives.[6]

We asked women what they would want in a job upon reentry. The number one answer was flexibility. Many describe wanting to retrain for a different kind of work. A former bank executive imagines becoming a teacher. A former dancer muses over becoming a physical therapist. These women argue that they want jobs that will offer flexibility and meaning. A former sales representative, now a part-time consultant, sums up the ideal described repeatedly by women in interviews: "To have an interesting, engaging, challenging role in an organization that I enjoy the people in, with a flexible schedule that can accommodate my investment into my family at a decent pay level. And, that has the potential to be a stepping-stone to continually position me for what I'm going to do when I grow up. The kids won't be around forever."

While few of those we interviewed indicated a desire to return to their former positions, many envisioned future work in the same field. These women plan to use their knowledge base and skill set to create flexible jobs in their fields, such as the former health-industry stock analyst who plans to consult with venture capital firms interested in medical technology start-ups. A practicing attorney wants to teach in a law school. A medical doctor wants to consult on public health issues. Another medical doctor wants to move to part-time clinical work and teaching in a medical school, instead of returning to full-time clinical work. Not wanting to return to the constraints and inflexibility they left behind in their prior jobs, some women describe having to create the jobs themselves. In effect, they describe joining a national trend of women moving into self-employment.

You Are Not the Boss of Me

Women have increased their self-employment rates by over one-quarter since the early 1980s, from 5.4 percent to 6.8 percent in 2003.[7] These women make up almost one-third of all self-employed workers, up from just under one-quarter in 1980. While much of that rise took place in the 1980s, the rates have picked up once again after a slight decline in the 1990s.[8] The numbers are even more striking when you consider majority women-owned firms (firms in which women own 51 percent or more of the company). According to the Center for Women's Business Research, in 2006, 30 percent of all privately held companies were majority women-owned, and these firms generated over $1 trillion in sales.[9]

The vast majority (69 percent) of women-owned firms operate in the service sector, 14 percent are retail operations, and 8 percent are related to real estate or the rental and leasing of goods.[10] Most of these firms do not hire employees. Of the 7.7 million privately held, majority women-owned firms, only 12.6 percent have employees, but these firms employ more than 7 million people.[11]

While some women we interviewed were only in the embryonic planning stages of starting their own businesses, others already were self-employed. Anxious to determine their own hours, clients, projects, and destiny, these women carved out space in their lives to start their own businesses. Maggie, for instance, met her husband while working at a large international corporation overseas. After they returned to the states, she worked at an Internet start-up company. While she was pregnant with her first child, her company went bust. With no firm to return to after the baby was born, she decided to try her hand at consulting instead of looking for a new job. Building upon her international knowledge and contacts, Maggie consulted for a small import business. This work suited Maggie because she made good use of her skills and could establish her own part-time hours. Now, she's launching a wholesale importing business. This enterprise will use her expertise and challenge her, but her work conditions will be on her own terms. "I chose wholesale because it will have flexible, family-friendly hours," she told us. And, best of all for Maggie, this will allow her the flexibility to work primarily during the hours her children are at school.

In addition to being able to manage their schedules, some women also sought the autonomy that self-employment can bring. Recall Kate, whom we met in chapter 4. After being squeezed out of her position at a start-up, Kate decided that she would never work for anyone else again: "I didn't want to be judged by other people's criteria for my success." She took four months off to develop a plan and then started her own consulting business, helping start-up companies to launch their businesses. She works out of her home, and limits her clients so she can set her own hours. While she now only works a limited number of hours, this solution allows her to attain her goal of maintaining a career trajectory while being at home. Kate's case is also interesting because it demonstrates what employers lose when they overlook the attributes of workers who, while unable to fit into the constraints of the traditional workplace, show extraordinary initiative, drive, ambition, and entrepreneurial spirit in being able to start their own business. This closer examination of the lives of women who feel pushed out of the workforce is powerful commentary on what the world of work loses when it fails to make a place for these women.

Yet while self-employment seems like an ideal solution to many women, in many cases, it is not as financially lucrative as working for an employer. Working outside the normative world of work can have its costs. Studies show that self-employed women earn less than equally qualified women who earn wages or salaries.[12] Also, health insurance is extremely costly for the self-employed, and these high costs can be prohibitive unless they can be covered under a spouse's health plan. Given these difficulties, many women who reenter the labor force want to work for an established business.

Getting Back on the Fast Track

In any case, whether reentering from a hiatus or trying to ramp up to a higher intensity career, as Mary Ann Mason and Eve Mason Ekman document, women who leave the fast track are unlikely to have the option to return to it.[13] As we noted in the previous sections, few of the women we interviewed expressed a desire to resume life on the fast track after having children. We want to be clear, however, that we believe that does not represent the views of all women. Some women do want to ride the crest of their career throughout their lives, to give voice to that "special gift" Eleanor Roosevelt described. Clearly there is a serious structural flaw with a system that does not give women the option of ramping back up if they are willing to devote the hours and the energy to do so. We agree with Mason and Ekman's assertion that a woman should have the option to use a part-time schedule when her children are young and the right to return to a full-time position after family obligations ease up. We would only add that these accommodations should extend to fathers as well as mothers, and that the flexibility to manage care needs at home not be limited to when one's children are young. Chapter 7 illustrated how these care needs might vary from family to family. By keeping the family, rather than the woman, as the unit of analysis, we can see that care needs at home transcend the caregiver's status as a parent. These distinctions are subtle, but important, because any one of us can face unexpected and compelling care responsibilities on the home front, and that reality is not bound by gender or parental status.

Changing Attitudes toward Sequencing Moms

Highly educated women who leave work for family reasons typically spend about two years out of the workforce before they try to reenter.[14] As increasing numbers of women "opt out," increasing numbers of women want to opt back in. Multiple resources have evolved to facilitate this transition, including specialized recruiting firms, "reentry" business-school programs, Web sites, books, and articles. Firms are also beginning to structure programs to retain women who choose to leave work for family reasons.

Changing demographics may be transforming the attitudes of employers toward reentering women. As the baby boomers begin to retire, firms will be faced with developing leaders from the "baby bust" generation, those between thirty-five and forty-five years old in 2008, which is precisely the age range of many women sequencing back into the workforce. Savvy firms recognize that there is a huge pool of underutilized talent among the women who have left the workforce for family reasons.

In addition to hiring sequencing women, employers are also creating policies to encourage women who leave to maintain a connection to the firms. Employers recognize the huge investment they make in their high-level employees, and losing women executives is incredibly costly in this respect. Estimates for the cost of replacing an executive run from one to two times the executive's salary. And these costs don't include the soft costs of knowledge loss or potential loss of clients.[15]

In response, some employers, such as PricewaterhouseCoopers and Deloitte & Touche, for instance, offer programs where employees may leave the firm for up to five years to focus on personal matters, including family. These employees can use company resources to keep their skills up to date and also receive firm-subsidized training. While there is no guarantee that these former employees will return to the company, of course that is the expectation. IBM, another woman-friendly firm, allows employees to take up to three years off, during which they may retain their health benefits and after which they have the option to return to work in either a full-time or part-time capacity. While the programs are open to men and women, and the reasons for opting into the program are not restricted to family, one of the main goals is to retain sequencing mothers.[16]

Reentry programs are not limited to corporations, however. Citing major attrition of female attorneys, law firms are also beginning to entertain reentry programs. Modeling the programs at PricewaterhouseCoopers and Deloitte & Touch, for example, the massive corporate law firm Skadden, Arps, Slate, Meagher & Flom allows attorneys a leave of absence for up to three years, during which time they maintain connections with the firm, with the expectation that they will return to the law firm at the end.[17] The American Bar Association developed a program, "Back to Business Law," to provide ongoing legal-education programs as well as networking opportunities for lawyers who leave their practices but intend to return in the future.[18]

Two examples illustrate the evolution of thought that is occurring in firms across the country. Anna, an attorney, decided to leave her practice to attend to a dying mother and new baby. Anna was considered to be a "star" associate, on the fast track to partnership at a large corporate law firm. Since the firm had no extended leave policy, Anna saw no alternative but to tender her resignation. After Anna announced her intention to quit, another associate, herself a mother of a preschooler, suggested to their boss that he give Anna an extended leave instead of letting her quit. Anna was such a valued employee, her boss wanted to do what he could to encourage her to return to their firm. He called the firm's CEO and requested permission to give Anna an extended, indefinite leave of absence. The firm had never granted an indefinite leave before, but the CEO readily agreed, in effect creating a new policy. Anna's story represents an individual case, yet it may be emblematic of a movement that is slowly taking root in the American workplace.

Serena, an environmental consultant who sequenced back into the labor force after a two-year hiatus at home with her son, described how she has served as an advocate at her firm for tapping into the pool of educated at-home moms as a potential labor force.

> I told them [the managing partners of her consulting firm]—they were three men—look around you, even within a few blocks of this build-

ing. Do you know how many talented women there are out there just dying to get a part-time gig? All you need to do is give them some flexibility and you'll be set. It's an enormous pool of talent. It was funny because I could tell they were starting to think about their own neighborhoods, and the woman next door or down the street. Oh, yeah, the light was dawning. So now we have a couple of writers and graphic designers working for us part-time.

Serena felt lucky. She got her job through a connection to a former classmate who knew her and was willing to take a chance on her. Once she was installed she was able to convince the firm to start thinking about systematizing what worked for her. What is interesting about these two examples is that in each case, the impetus for change at the workplace was jumpstarted by a working mother. Similarly, the case of Google we presented in chapter 6 revolved around the initiation of an in-house child care policy that coincided with a vice president for product management's return to work from maternity leave.[19] Of course, in all of these cases, the men in leadership positions were amenable to changing policy, because the women who initiated the policy change were themselves a part of the company's power structure. And this, in turn, bodes well for individual women to create these types of arrangements with their employers, as the culture of expectations at the workplace appears set to change.

The Age of Turbulence

We have examined the challenges of reentry in the context of a growing economy, but they expand exponentially in economic slowdowns. Economic turbulence leads many employers to enter into a bunker mentality of sorts, and so reentering the workforce during a deep recession becomes even more challenging. With large numbers of jobs destroyed and so many people made redundant, the competition for open positions can be fierce. Women who want to reenter the workforce in times of recession will have a more difficult time negotiating family-friendly policies, as so many people are clamoring for the jobs and are willing to do whatever it takes to keep the jobs they have.

As firms try to cut costs wherever they can, family-friendly, flexible policies are likely to be among the first on the chopping block. For some, policies may be cut completely, for others, perhaps just whittled back. But some flexible policies, such as telecommuting, can actually make firms more cost-efficient. Telecommuting reduces overhead and increases productivity and retention. Job sharing, when done correctly, gives firms the benefit of two minds. In addition, forward-thinking firms should recognize the power of maintaining or even creating more flexible options for workers as a way to position themselves for the recovery. So while reentry during recession may be difficult or even impossible, when the economy recovers it is likely that flexible work options will once again be a tool that firms use to attract and retrain workers.

Workers consistently rank flexibility as a characteristic they look for in a job, and there is no reason to think that this preference will shift when we return to a period of economic expansion. In light of that, Wharton management professor Nancy Rothbard offers another reason why firms may not cut back on flexible policies by as much as one might expect during a downturn. Companies want to maintain their position on lists such as *Fortune*'s "Best Companies to Work For," and one way to do that is to retain flexible work policies.[20] Which policies are kept or cut will depend on the firm and on the depth of the recession.

Business Schools, Recruiting Firms, and the At-Home Mom

Business schools, always on the lookout for new ways to market their products, have noted the large pool of reentering professionals in need of "refresher" courses. In response, several elite business schools have recently developed programs tailored to reentering professionals. In 2006, the Tuck School of Business at Dartmouth launched a career reentry program called "Back in Business." Run over the course of three weekends, this executive program is designed to facilitate the reentry of professionals into the workplace.

Tuck admits women and men who already have MBAs (or who have MBA-equivalent experience) as well as "work experience in a high-potential career." While admission to the program is gender neutral, Tuck expects that women sequencing back into work will be the primary target audience.[21] This program for former high-powered executives charges close to seven thousand dollars for tuition, room, and board for the twelve-day session. Other business schools, such as Harvard and Stanford, have followed Tuck's lead in offering executive education leadership programs for women.

In 2007, Wharton's executive education program launched "Career Comeback: A UBS Fellowship Program for Professional Women Re-entering the Workforce." Designed specifically for women with graduate degrees and a minimum of five years of experience, Wharton distinguishes itself by offering the program as a fellowship: with UBS, a major financial services firm, underwriting the program, participants pay no tuition. Not surprisingly, this program is quite competitive, and the first two classes quickly filled to capacity.

Business schools are also targeting women who do not already have an MBA. Pepperdine University was the first to offer a part-time, "morning MBA" program geared specifically for stay-at-home moms in 2006. DePaul University launched a similar program in 2007, and one can expect that more business schools will follow suit.

Business schools are not the only organizations trying to capitalize on the reentry challenges facing women. Employers view returning women in a better light than they did in the past because they want to draw from the pool of reentering professional women. Sequencing moms want to return to these firms, but in more flexible positions than the ones they left. Seeing a market for their services, recruiting firms have emerged, specializing in placing workers in flexible work arrangements. Recruiting firms, such as On-Ramps Services and Mom Corps, argue that companies can increase profits by making flexibility a cornerstone of their recruiting and retention policies. These recruiters market their ability to provide firms with access to the large pool of highly skilled workers who want flexibility. These specialized search firms attract reentering women by offering a "jumpstart" to people who have left the workforce for family reasons.

There are a multitude of Web-based resources for sequencing mothers. Web sites with tips for mothers on how to reenter the labor force abound. These free sites give advice on how to handle résumé gaps (write a skills-based, not a chronological, résumé), how to stay connected while on leave (take on small consulting jobs), and how to volunteer strategically (do volunteer work that allows you to demonstrate appropriate skills upon reentry).

Women interested in sequencing can also find support groups. One of the most famous, Mothers & More, is a nonprofit organization that was formed to address the needs of sequencing mothers. The group has over eight thousand members with 175 local chapters that provide support, social events, and even play dates for moms and their children. And there is no shortage of books to help guide sequencing moms. Recent titles include *Back on the Career Track: A Guide for Stay-at-Home Moms Who Want to Return to Work*, by Carol Fishman Cohen and Vivian Steir Rabin, and *Comeback Moms: How to Leave Work, Raise Children, and Restart Your Career Even if You Haven't Had a Job in Years*, by Monica Samuels and J. C. Conklin.

Challenging economic times aside, it may take some time for trendsetting policies to take hold. Take, for example, policies of hiring part-time workers. One of the reasons firms give for not hiring part-time workers relates to the client expectations of immediate access to their consultants, lawyers, or investment bankers. Client expectations are difficult to change, but there is precedence. In the not-too-distant past, women expected "their doctor" to deliver their babies. This expectation led to a life of frequent overnight call for obstetricians. As women entered the OB/GYN subspecialties in large numbers, they began to alter patient expectations. It is rare to find an OB today who will commit to delivering her patient's baby. Patients are told to schedule prenatal visits with all the doctors in a practice, so that she will have at least met the doctor who eventually delivers her child.

As we highlighted at the start of this chapter, not all women who leave their careers for home choose to return to work. For those who do want to return, this chapter has described some of the realities of reentry, in good economic times and bad, and given strategies for how to get back to work. In the following chapter we explore the creative strategies that employed women use to balance work and family.

CHAPTER THIRTEEN

Creative Strategies
for Making Work "Work"

All around the country, the women were waking up.
MEG WOLITZER, *The Ten-Year Nap*, 2008

Women are resourceful, and whether they work full-time, part-time, or according to some other arrangement, they employ creative strategies to manage their situations. For the most part, women herald flexibility as the number one job characteristic to help them balance work and family. Flexibility can take many forms, with varying benefits to the employee, including reduced hours, flexible start and end times, and telecommuting. Flexible work arrangements do not necessarily equate to part-time work, however. A flexible employer might require a full-time work commitment, but allow the work to be done outside of the office or during nonstandard work hours. Earlier we explored the lives of at-home moms; here we focus on the strategies women use to balance paid work and family. These strategies include sequencing, reducing work hours, forgoing advancements at work, reprioritizing nonwork time, choosing to live in family-friendly communities, and, for those who continue to "hit it hard" at work—making the most of flexible work arrangements.

Sequencing: Having It All, Just Not All at Once

Feeling torn between their careers and their families, some women feel that they just can't do the quality of work they expect of themselves and have the family life they desire at the same time. Not wanting to "just get by" either at work or at home, for some of these women, sequencing career and family is a way around the quandary. Coined in the late 1980s by Arlene Cardozo, "sequencing" has come to be understood as a way that women can balance work and family by ordering or "sequencing" child-raising and career.[1] Cardozo's argument of "having it all, just not all at once" has gained traction in the past decade, resonating with American women who want to spend time as an at-home mom without losing their professional identities.

Sequencing can be accomplished in different ways. In one sequence, a woman might focus on family concerns while in her twenties and then begin her career after the children have gone to school. Famous examples of women who have successfully navigated this type of sequencing include former secretary of state Madeleine Albright, the first woman to hold that office and at that time the highest-ranking woman in the history of the United States government; Sandra Day O'Connor, the first female Supreme Court justice; and Speaker of the House of Representatives Nancy Pelosi, the first woman to lead an American political party. An alternative sequence might entail finishing college and graduate school, pushing forward on a career, and then once established, leaving work to tend to family. Once the children are older, this sequence continues with a return to the paid labor force.

Of course, women's lives are more complicated than the black-and-white description of these sequences. Some work full-time when their children are small and then sequence home when the children reach middle school. Others continue to keep some attachment to work even when "at home" by doing freelance or consulting work. In fact, the concept of sequencing has evolved to include women who reduce work hours to part-time or change careers for family reasons, in addition to those who quit their job. That said, most of the women in our study fall into this second type of sequencing—women who established their careers first, and then sequenced home.

Reducing Hours at Work

Sequencing is not always a feasible or desirable option. For these women an obvious way to relieve the stresses associated with juggling a high-powered career and a family is to reduce the time spent at work. These reductions might include eliminating overtime, such as the woman who reported, "I still work full-time, but now I work forty hours per week instead of sixty-plus." Others move from full-time to part-time positions, and the designs of part-time arrangements vary widely. Firms are now more likely to have part-time options for their employees than ever before. One lawyer credits her law firm for providing "excellent flexibility to work on various part-time schedules for many years at 80 percent of a full-time equivalent while advancing professionally. Still a lot of hours, but flexibility is the key to success." This attorney hits on a key point that flexibility without a penalty is critical for women who want to continue to advance in their professions.

The possible penalties for moving to a part-time status are serious, as we detail in chapters 4 and 10. Nevertheless, it seems that increasing numbers of working moms wish they could work part-time, at least during some points in their lives, while full-time work has become less appealing. Women's attitudes have changed in the past decade with respect to their "ideal" work-family balance. A 2007 Pew Research Center survey found that only 21 percent of working mothers of children under eighteen say that full-time work is their ideal, down from 32 percent in 1997. And four in five mothers who work part-time believe they have achieved their ideal work status.[2] Almost half of at-home mothers reported that being home was their ideal situation, and about a third indicated that they would prefer to be working part-time. Full-time work is not appealing to this group. Only 16 percent of at-home moms reported they would prefer to be working full-time, down from 25 percent in 2007. Dads, on the other hand, feel differently. Almost three-quarters of men with children under eighteen say that working full-time is their ideal situation. And more would prefer not to work outside the home (16 percent) over working part-time (12 percent).[3]

Some fields are more amenable to part-time work than others. Medicine, for example, seems to allow for part-time more easily than law. Women are most likely to take advantage of the part-time policies, when available. For example, among graduating pediatric residents, more than half of the females, as compared to 15 percent of their male counterparts, indicated they plan to arrange for a part-time position within five years of completing their residency.[4] At 26 percent, pediatrics leads specialties in the number of part-time physicians. The ability of female physicians to negotiate part-time arrangements and to retain a right to return to full-time work when their caregiving responsibilities at home diminish may be a primary reason that women do not opt out of the medical field as readily as women in law, who are less likely to have this option.[5]

Forgoing Opportunities to Advance at Work

While much is made of women's decisions to reduce to part-time or even to leave the workforce entirely, a strategy that is used far more often goes undetected because it's so hard to identify—choosing a particular type of job with the expectation of enjoying a less-hectic family life. Some choose careers with family balance specifically in mind. Almost half of the married mothers in our survey sample, for example, indicated that they considered family balance issues when choosing a job, identifying location, flexibility, hours per week, and kind of job as primary influences in their choice of job.

One woman reported that she took jobs in the nonprofit sector "partly because they provide more flexibility and 'life outside the job' even though you make less money than in the private sector." These women are quite matter-of-fact when they describe their decision-making process for choosing jobs that were something less than their ideal job. A teacher sums it up: "I didn't select education as my dream job—I selected it as my security job. I had other more adventurous jobs, more stimulating jobs, and more unpredictable jobs. But I settled into teaching when I started my family because I knew I couldn't continue as before. I learned to create the adventure within my final chosen career."

Another woman said, "In order to better parent, I have stayed beyond the time I would have liked to in this position." This quote illustrates a common strategy that bubbled to the surface again and again in our interviews. Multiple women describe forgoing advancements within their current jobs. One woman said that on the basis of family considerations, she stopped trying to get promoted: "But I still did my job and accepted everything thrown at me. I just stopped trying to grab more." Some women turned down outside job offers, such as Jill, who said, "Since getting pregnant two years ago, I have made a conscious effort to lessen my load at work and have turned down enticing job offers in favor of staying at a 'safe' job where my work ethic is not questioned and I have lots of flexibility and support." Another describes making "horizontal moves in my career to achieve better hours or a more flexible shift for my family." All of these iterations of forgoing opportunities to advance at work can be seen as strategies women (and men) use to better negotiate the realities of work and family.

Managing Priorities

Managing priorities arose as a common strategy employed by women who combine work and family. In particular, women described how reorienting the way they spend their time allowed for much greater satisfaction and far less stress. By reducing time spent on housework, community service, or commuting, these women created space for a work and family balance that fits their family's needs.

Similar to the point we raised in chapter 7, one way women find ways to spend more time with their kids is by reducing the amount of time spent on housework. Being willing to "let things slide" at home frees up a woman's discretionary time during a given week. If things heat up at work at the same time that your daughter's softball team goes to state and she *really* wants you there to support her, you can skip cooking and let the bathroom stay grubby. One working mom put it this way: "Every time you're in a bit of a pinch, just lower the bar. Just lower it until it's on the ground because, you know, as long as you've got your priorities—you know, the few, the handful of what's important—then everything else just isn't that critical. Balls are dropping all over the place. You just have to figure out which ones are important and which aren't."

Reprioritizing time also means forgoing activities outside of work and family. While they would like to volunteer, some women feel that the only way to "make it all work" is to say no to requests for outside activities. "I'm not doing community-oriented work. I'd like to, but it would come now at the expense of homework with the kids, riding bikes, etc. Right now, selfishly, I'm like a mama bear. There will be time later to do these other things."

Reducing Commute Time and Telecommuting

Women also reprioritize time by reducing hours spent commuting. Traveling to and from work is a major time suck. The average American worker commutes about twenty-four minutes each way, per day. That sounds like a reasonable commute. But when you add it up, you find that over the course of a year American workers spend over one hundred hours commuting.[6] That's twenty hours more than the two weeks of vacation a typical worker takes each year. Imagine gaining an additional two weeks of time with your kids, at your job, at the gym, or on a date with your partner. Women who feel pressed for time report that hours spent commuting were precious time wasted. It's no wonder then that reducing or even eliminating that commute surfaced as a major strategy women use to "make it all work."

Many of the women we surveyed rearranged their work lives to minimize commuting time. One described how increased commuting time led her to switch jobs: "My travel to work had increased from twenty to thirty-four miles, which is one of the reasons I quit. Now I work two miles from home." Another said, "I looked for jobs that did not require working outside the town where we live. I did not want to commute." And reducing time spent commuting to nonwork activities also arose as a strategy: "I make sure I'm close to home (school, work, activities, church). We don't waste time getting places. I don't have a commuter mentality." And, instead of getting a job close to home, one woman described moving to a house closer to her job and choosing a child care facility that was also close to home.

Telecommuting provides the ultimate reduction in commute time, cutting it to the minutes it takes to walk to the home office. Women who transitioned to telecommuting full-time reflected on the isolation, but ultimately were willing to trade off the companionship of co-workers for the extra time telecommuting afforded them: "Now that I work from home, I miss having an office and interacting with co-workers. I'd love to be in an office, but I wouldn't if it meant commuting an hour each way." Women also use telecommuting as a strategy to keep their jobs after relocating for their husband's job. One woman, who was tired of changing jobs each time her husband's work moved them overseas, commented, "I was going to change jobs once again, but my employer offered to let me work 100 percent from home. I now have a job I can do anywhere that a high-speed Internet connection is available."

Some of the women we surveyed fully telecommuted for their jobs, but many more negotiated to telecommute one to two days per week. By agreeing to a partial telecommute, the employers were able to retain highly productive workers, who otherwise might have left their positions. For many of these women, partial telecommuting served as a compromise between working full-time and part-time, or as a way to negotiate around a lengthy commute. "I'm working full-time but in the sense that I am telecommuting about two days a week. And then the three days I do go into the office I do have a pretty big commute." Reducing the time spent getting to and from the office, therefore, gave women the additional minutes they needed each week to manage work and home.

Where You Live Can Make All the Difference

Choosing where to live presents an effective strategy for balancing work and family. Many women we interviewed made location decisions primarily based on where they thought it would be best to raise their families. Some women purposefully chose to live in communities that would provide a better living environment for their children, despite the toll that such a move would take on their careers: "My current job doesn't offer me some of the advancement opportunities that I would have in a larger community/city, nor does it offer me the choices of work that I would have in a larger office/city. That is fine. It is more important to me to live in a place where I am comfortable raising my children . . . than to have the 'perfect' or 'most satisfying' job." Others credit the family-friendliness of their communities: "I live in a small mountain town that particularly values children, and feel that has much to do with the fact that I found a job that allows me to have a family and keep life balanced." And, while the notion of a family-friendly community can seem ideologically tinged and can bump up against the politically polemical idea of "family values," there is substance to the claim that some places can be more child-friendly than others. Anthropologist Meredith Small points out that "we live in a culture with a low birthrate" and that in many ways "we live in an antichild culture." With this observation, she is making the point that in other countries where there are more children around, children are more a part of daily life.[7] And by choosing to live in places where children's presence is the norm more than the exception, people are seeking a more supportive environment.

A more intense version of this can be seen in living near family. Living close to family networks can help enormously with parenting, especially for couples where one often travels on overnight trips. Christy, whose husband travels several nights per week, reflected on the critical role her sister played through the years. "When our kids were little . . . in the middle of the night I'd hear a noise, I'd have my sister right there, and she'd come over. You know, in the middle of the night I'm smelling gas, and so then I'd load up the kids and off we'd go over to Laurie's house. And so she was like having another husband . . . she filled in for Adrian when he was gone. And so that's enormously huge, huge, huge."

Operating a Small Business

For many women, a strategy for getting around the constraints of "working for the man" was to strike out on their own. As we detailed in chapter 12, women are becoming increasingly entrepreneurial. Self-employed women cite the ability to set their own hours as one of the major benefits of their work arrangement. In fact, many of the women we surveyed turned to self-employment specifically as a way to create their own part-time work experience when they were blocked by their former employers. A former human resources executive recounted, "My boss at my last job refused part-time hours, so that immediately made me quit full-out. I then worked one to two hours a week on the side for the family business. A year later I launched a business but have always maintained my mom mode first."

Self-employment on a part-time basis also helps women who plan to return to full-time employment in the future to fill their résumé gaps. One woman, who has started up two Web site ventures with her father since leaving her job, believes that the skills she's developed will translate well if she moves back into a corporate environment: "I definitely think that it's a struggle for women to have a gap in employment because you're forced to either say I was a stay-at-home mom or sort of hope that the employer doesn't notice, but of course they will. But in my case, I've actually added skills, huge skills, that would actually be beneficial to an employer."

Work Hard, Play Hard

In much of this book, we have addressed issues women face when they combine paid work and raising families. With all this attention to the impediments families, and in particular women, face uniting home and career, one might question how women with kids are ever successful. Yet, some are tremendously successful. In *Mothers on the Fast Track: How a New Generation Can Balance Family and Careers*, Mason and Ekman identify time management, knowing when to say no, and controlling what they refer to as "mother guilt" as key strategies of women who manage to balance family and fast-track careers.[8] With this analysis, they are reinforcing themes we have discussed at length in this chapter. We also identified another key factor to a mother's success in a high-charged career: an excellent support system at home. Whether that support system came in the form of a live-in nanny, a mother-in-law, or a stay-at-home spouse, not having to worry about how things were managed at home seems to be critical to a working mother's ability to maintain her position.

ᴵᴺᴵᴺᴵᴺ (decorative)

Coming of Age in America

You have brains in your head.
You have feet in your shoes.
You can steer yourself any direction you choose.

DR. SEUSS, OH, THE PLACES YOU'LL GO! 1990

Title VII of the Civil Rights Act of 1964 made it illegal for employers to discriminate on the basis of race, color, religion, national origin, or sex. This important legislation ushered in broad societal changes. Before the 1970s, women had little room to maneuver in choosing their future occupation. A few headstrong types have always slipped through, but it was only a generation ago that we started to see a critical mass of women looking askance when their high school guidance counselor attempted to steer them toward pursuing studies in fields traditionally dominated by women, such as home economics, nursing, or elementary education. Instead, a generation of women intently fixed their collective gaze somewhere on the horizon, far beyond their guidance counselor's office. A tipping point was reached when these young women quietly, but determinedly, set their sights on following in the footsteps of the likes of Sandra Day O'Connor, Geraldine Ferraro, Mae Jemison, or Madeleine Albright and subsequently embarked on careers in law, medicine, business, science, government, and beyond.

This is not the generation of women who, in the 1960s and 1970s, supposedly burned their bras. Rather, this is the generation of women who, in the 1980s and 1990s, bought jogging bras, and stride by steady stride, proceeded to keep pace with men, making significant inroads into the old boys' network. Clad in shoulder-padded suits, these women set about to avoid bias by mastering the cultural rules for excelling in a man's world. Hour by billable hour, they proved their worth to firms and cemented women's hard-won advances toward gender equality in the workplace.

These women, therefore, are not necessarily the generation who will go down in the history books as America's "firsts"—the first female U.S. Supreme Court justice, the first female vice-presidential candidate, the first African American woman astronaut, the first woman secretary of state. They are, however, the ones who sustained the momentum of the steady rise in women's labor force participation rates, ascent in institutions of higher education, and increasing representation in the boardroom, the courtroom, and the operating room. These women, if not the thin edge of the wedge that first inserted itself between the gates of the bastions of male privilege, are surely the ones who applied the unrelenting pressure that ultimately crashed those gates.

In this book, we have explored what lay beyond those gates and how these women who collectively crashed them are faring as they attempt to combine paid work and motherhood. Our analysis spans the breadth of the twentieth century to the present, but we single out post–civil rights era college-educated women for special consideration, documenting the lives of both those who are employed for pay and those who stay home with their children. These women represent a particularly rich and fascinating part of the transforming landscape of gender and work in America for a variety of reasons.

Women in this age group dominate female labor force participation in America. Folk singer Helen Reddy's vision of "numbers too big to ignore" has been realized. Nowadays, women make up almost half of the U.S. labor force, with six in ten women working for pay. How, where, when, and whether this segment of the population participates in the labor force has significant implications for our economy as a whole. Issues of gender and work in America are no longer about so-called women's lib, but about how our society as a whole is going to progress and to remain competitive on a global stage.

The educational profile of women in this age group also makes them compelling. These women represent the largest-ever cohort of college-educated women in America. The increases in women's educational levels over the past thirty years are nothing short of stunning. The number of American women who hold college degrees more than tripled between 1970 and 2007. And, as we have detailed, women in their midtwenties to early thirties are more educated than their male counterparts.

Similarly, we have documented women's phenomenal rise at work in recent decades. Women born in the decade or so after World War II represent the first large wave of women to compete for prominent positions in the U.S. labor force. These women's entry into the labor force resulted in unprecedented strides in women's representation in the workplace.

Yet all the while, elements of the perfect storm were gathering on the horizon. We live in a society that treats children as pets, placing the full burden of raising the next generation squarely on the shoulders of the nuclear family. As we have noted, parents who raise the next generation of workers create extraordinary value for society at large with little to no support from government or firms. This dynamic is illustrated in the enduring inadequacies of child care options for working parents, obliging families to rely on very costly and often ad hoc measures to care for their children while they are at work.

While women, like horses out of the gate, surged ahead at school when finally presented with the opportunity to prove themselves academically, at the same time, marriage patterns were shifting. To paraphrase Gloria Steinem, these women were becoming the men they wanted to marry. And this dynamic produced another wrinkle. When two professionals marry, this gives rise to something we call "the 100-hour couple," or a couple where the husband and wife work extremely long hours for a combined total of well over one hundred hours per week. As many of these women were competing for professional and managerial positions (and married men who were doing the same), we began to see a surge in the hours employers expected professionals to devote to work. The higher one climbs the income ladder, the more hours one works. And because women are fitting into a work structure designed by and for men, few alternatives exist to facilitate combining work and motherhood. For example, few careers have options that allow women time to devote to family for a period of their lives and then resume upward mobility in their careers on a par with their male colleagues who are parents. We have shown how women shattered glass ceilings, only to be confronted with maternal walls.

All of this coincides with ongoing cultural shifts in expectations for parenthood. While dads are spending more time than ever with their children, we see the intensification of motherhood, measured in what women we interviewed call "mama time." All of this is compounded by enduring expectations for women to be in charge of the home, if not doing the actual cleaning then managing the paid workers who do so.

Some were surprised when this perfect storm broke at the turn of the twenty-first century. Women, professionals in particular, started leaving their jobs. Women had always cycled in and out of the labor force, but this time it was different. The prominence of the positions the women held, the number of women doing it, and the media coverage this phenomenon generated coalesced to make this a "hot" issue. The actual number of women who left their jobs to care for children around this time constituted a minority of working women, but still it precipitated a maelstrom of public debate, becoming a lightning rod issue in the culture wars.

Drawn in by the controversial nature of the debate, we began our research by telescoping in on the lives of women who had quit their jobs. We soon discovered that the more compelling part of this story, however, is how those who walked away from careers, high powered and otherwise, reveal issues faced by all women who seek to combine paid work and childrearing. Our research then evolved to account for this expanded scope. Peering into the lives of elite at-home moms who employ nannies to raise the children and staff to run the home has a certain voyeuristic appeal. Yet it is the stories of lament from bright, well-educated, promising women who couldn't see a path forward in combining work and family that we found so poignant and so troubling. One forty-year-old told us, "I never worked after college. I went straight to graduate school, earned my PhD and started as a post doc. I left my position as a research scientist because I realized that that life was incompatible with my version of family." And it was ultimately the stories of these young scientists, attorneys, and academics, who felt stymied in their efforts to make use of their "great gift for some particular thing" while not giving up "the joy of marrying and having a home and children," that propelled us forward in our quest to understand the forces that were shaping contemporary women's lives.[1] How had so much changed, yet so little changed in the three-quarters of a century since Eleanor Roosevelt first voiced this concern?

In October 2008, Lisa Belkin, the journalist who first coined the phrase "opting out" in 2003, signed off after nine years of writing a *New York Times* column on work-life issues, concluding that "there were no answers—just endless and penetrating questions."[2] Belkin's realization echoes our aim with this book—not to tell women what they should be doing with their lives in terms of work and family—but to chart a path through the complexity of it all, presenting the options, the trade-offs, the realities, and the ideals.

One dimension of the complexity of gender, work, and identity can be seen in our interviews with women who continue to juggle careers and children. Many of those we interviewed in their midthirties to late forties describe being "blindsided" by the realities of juggling career and children. These women were told they could "do it all." Some described pursuing a career based more on what they knew they did not want—to be a "homemaker" like their mom or to be an assistant to someone with more credentials than they had or to "ghostwrite" and to let someone else take credit for their ideas—than on any clear career pathway of a particular mentor or role model. Of course, it is hard to look to a role model if no mentors exist. In many fields, very few women had already moved up the ladder, and when they had, not many were mothers. Therefore, few of these younger women were trained or mentored by women who had successfully negotiated combining paid work and raising children themselves.[3] This wave of women was, therefore, not well informed about the constraints inherent in juggling job and family.

Jen, a copy editor, who completed her bachelor's degree in 1985, observed: "When we were in college nobody thought about career and family. We thought about getting married and having careers. I don't remember anybody ever talking about, you know, how you are going to arrange your life." Melissa, a former marketing executive in the recording industry, who graduated high school in 1982, describes what she calls a superwoman phenomenon: "The eighties really did a mind job on all of us in terms of expectations of what women should achieve. . . . That's a hard stream to swim against. The old mentality that was so engrained in us . . . the concept of the superwoman in the eighties was . . . something that was thrown in our faces constantly."

This concept of the superwoman archetype was anchored in popular culture of the time. Some women in this age group mused about how they remembered television shows from the 1970s, like *Wonder Woman*, starring Lynda Carter, as a fictional superheroine; *Isis*, starring Joanna Cameron, as a young high school science teacher; and Lindsay Wagner as the Bionic Woman. All of these fictional characters advanced the notion that women are poised, prepared, and powerfully equipped to take on the world. It is only in retrospect that women considered that all of these icons, while smart and strong (not to mention gorgeous), were also single and childless.

Beyond these fictional characters, however, Melissa and Jen raise many themes that we've discussed in this book. In particular, we highlighted the disjuncture between how society attempts to frame mothers' decisions to leave or reduce their participation in the labor force and how women, themselves, see their experience. We endeavored to include how women frame their decision by looking at how parenthood pulls women home, at the extremely tight constraints they work within when they live in a household with fluidly competing demands of two jobs and children, and, finally, at how women have responded to society's attempts to categorize them by categorizing back through their professionalization of motherhood.

This superwoman notion is, perhaps, tellingly summarized by comedienne Lily Tomlin, who quipped, "If I had known what it was like to have it all, I might have settled for less."[4] Indeed, "having it all" remains an area of conflict for the women we interviewed. In this book, we have amply documented how harried and beleaguered many women who are juggling work and raising children feel. In concluding and in thinking about where this all will lead, it is important to ask critical questions about what we have described. Does realizing one's potential at work, having a life of the mind, and making a contribution to society have to be seen in opposition to having a family? Why is this question asked of women, but not of men?

Throughout this study, we've been mindful of the two parallel tracks that the women we studied followed: One led them to college, maybe graduate school, and then career. The other led to joining with a partner to form a family and bring up children. Katherine, one of the women we interviewed, called this metaphor into question when she told us,

Maybe the questions and the type of problems being posed have a tendency to be very lineal. Think about a life that develops along a line: You graduate from college and then you're building a career. You're building a family and everything kind of goes along a line. But I suppose when I think about experiencing my life, I'm more struck as years go by that life really isn't a line. It is really a kind of circling around, returning, coming back, setting out again, coming around, coming back. [laugh] More like a spiral. I did not really experience a lineal thing. I think I look back on my life progression more in this circular sort of a way, and also that maybe combining family and career [needs] to be seen [as] more of a kind of a moving back and forth between different needs and these two quite conflicted areas of life in many ways. I guess from my own experience you need to have that motion of circling around your life as a whole, instead of thinking of two lines that are parallel or going off in different directions.

Living life in a spiral is not problematic, per se. But, as Katherine pointed out, the work world works fairly lineally, as demonstrated in the chapters that covered the wage penalty women face when leaving the workforce or reducing their effort at work. When these women had children, their spiraling lives intersected with the linear demands of the workplace. The flexibility of the employer was crucial at these times. If the employer was able to bend to the needs of the employee at key points in the life cycle, the company retained dedicated and talented employees. If not, the woman either walked away—taking her education, her experience, and her potential to help the company grow with her—or, she settled into a position that underutilized her skills and potential, without a possibility of getting back on track.

There is no hard and fast line of demarcation among the women we interviewed in terms of age and approach to questions of work and family. In general, though, the youngest women we interviewed, in their twenties and early thirties, seem to approach questions of work and family somewhat differently than the women just older than them. It appears they have been watching carefully, and have learned some valuable lessons. We dub these women the "pragmatists." These women seem more realistic than older women about the competing demands of work and family. Samantha, a twenty-five-year-old working long hours and traveling a lot for her job in advertising, described her plans to have career and kids sequentially: "God, I watched my mom work so hard to manage having me and build her career. I'm not doing that. I don't plan to work after I have kids." These "pragmatists" are still gunning for top spots educationally, but they report being more mindful than the waves of women before them about how to negotiate career and family. While the superwomen were surprised by the difficulties of managing a demanding career and a sane family life, the pragmatists are planning for it.

These young women describe selecting a career that will be more flexible and amenable to the demands of child rearing. Others plan to have a career first, and then have children, while some intend to have children first and move into a career at some undefined future point when their children are older. Still others are counting on policies at work shifting to better accommodate their desire to negotiate both work and family.

Our finding that work-life balance is increasingly important to this younger age group was supported by a recent study by the Aspen Institute Center for Business Education of male and female MBA students at fifteen business schools. This study reported that "work-life balance" was the third most important factor for MBA students, following "challenging responsibilities" and "compensation."[5]

When one considers all the problems that beset our society today at home and abroad, it seems foolhardy to fail to accommodate the undertapped resource of capable, educated women with kids. Underusing this resource presents a huge inefficiency in our economy. Employers would benefit from the skills that these women would bring to their enterprises and women want to provide their talents, so why can't we seem to make it work? Economists recognize that these types of inefficiencies typically result from market failures. They expect that in the absence of a structural problem, markets will clear—in other words, the wage will adjust until the supply of workers equals the demand for workers. When markets clear, there is no wasted labor; there are no workers who would be willing to work at the market wage but are unable to get jobs. In the case of highly educated moms, the market doesn't clear—the current structure of the American workplace causes the labor market for these women to fail. These are qualified individuals who, given the appropriate flexibility, would like to work and would like to pursue careers commensurate with their training, but the way that work is structured prevents them from fully realizing their potential at work and, for those who take time off, blocks their return to the appropriate jobs given their skill levels.

While we are not yet in a position where the youngest cohort of women we've described is holding the economy hostage until they get what they want—and thus we do not see a revolution at hand—we do, however, see significant shifts in what a growing proportion of them are willing to sacrifice to get ahead at work. And, what makes this particularly potent as a possible signal of change is that some dads are starting to join the ranks of those clamoring for more accommodation of the compelling needs of home. Some hypothesize that the biggest contribution of this millennial generation—both men and women—will be to transform the culture at work. When the economy eventually bounces back and the markets for skilled labor tightens, employers who want to attract and retain these women will have to design work policies that will better accommodate the spiraling nature of women's lives.

Notes

Introduction

1. Cohany and Sok, "Trends in Labor Force Participation of Married Mothers of Infants."

2. Authors' calculation, U.S. Bureau of Census, Current Population Survey, Merged Outgoing Rotation Groups, various years.

3. The USDA also estimates that families making over $77,100 will spend $298,680 on average, while low-income families who earn less than $45,800 can expect to spend $148,320. U.S. Department of Agriculture, *Expenditures on Children by Families*, 2007.

4. Folbre, *Invisible Heart*.

5. Mason and Ekman, *Mothers on the Fast Track*.

6. Williams and Segal, "Beyond the Maternal Wall."

7. Forster, "Pregnancy Bias Claims Increase."

8. Bureau of Labor Statistics, American Time Use Survey 2006 News Release.

9. See, for example, Bennetts, *Feminine Mistake*.

10. Mason and Ekman, *Mothers on the Fast Track*.

One. Numbers Too Big to Ignore

1. To be considered part of the labor force, one must be at least sixteen years of age and either working, seeking employment, awaiting recall to a job, or waiting to start a new job. The labor force participation rate for the population is defined as the number of people in the labor force divided by the number of people over the age of fifteen. Persons in the military or incarcerated are not included in these statistics. Most of the reported historical labor force statistics use this measure of the labor force, although before 1970 the definition also included fifteen-year-olds. While it is possible to find labor force statistics for different age categories for more recent years, for consistency we use the standard definition.

2. Sources for the data in this section include Goldin, *Understanding the Gender Gap*; Blau, Ferber, and Winkler, *Economics of Women, Men, and Work*; and U.S. Bureau of Census, *2008 Statistical Abstract*, Table 584.

3. Bureau of Labor Statistics, *Databases, Tables, and Calculators*.

4. For example, a woman who sewed clothes for her family may have taken a job sewing clothes in a factory. This movement certainly changed her work status from unpaid to paid, but did not fundamentally alter the work that she did.

5. Bureau of Labor Statistics, "Employment Projections."

6. Goldin, *Understanding the Gender Gap*.

7. Bureau of Labor Statistics, *Women in the Labor Force: A Databook 2007*.

8. Coontz, *Way We Never Were*.

9. Ibid.

10. Goldin, *Understanding the Gender Gap*, 12.

11. Van Horn and Schaffner, *Work in America*.

12. Coontz, *Way We Never Were*.

13. We note here that this could more accurately be modified to say married *white* women of a certain economic standing. Patricia Hill Collins in *Black Feminist Thought* describes the racialized elements of this commonly held understanding.

14. Goldin, *Understanding the Gender Gap*, 6.

15. Blau, Ferber, and Winkler, *Economics of Women, Men, and Work*; U.S. Bureau of Census, *2008 Statistical Abstract of the United States*, Table 584.

16. Coontz, *Way We Never Were*.

17. Bureau of Labor Statistics, *Databases, Tables, and Calculators*, Historical A Tables.

18. U.S. Bureau of Census, *2008 Statistical Abstract of the United States*, Table 578 and Table 580.

19. Coontz, *Way We Never Were*.

20. The term "white-collar" arose to describe the class of jobs that generally do not require employees to wear work clothes or any type of protective clothing. Typically, white-collar jobs are office jobs, while "blue-collar" refers to factory or manual labor. Pink-collar jobs, on the other hand, are jobs that are typically dominated by women.

21. Goldin, *Understanding the Gender Gap*.

22. In addition to discrimination, Title VII also prohibits sexual harassment, which includes not only demands for sexual favors, but also creating a hostile environment. The original draft of Title VII did not include sex as a protected class. Ironically, an opponent of the Civil Rights Act added sex as a way to have the bill defeated. Hersch, "Employment Discrimination, Economists and the Law." Other important legislation includes the Equal Pay Act of 1963 (which mandated that men and women who do equivalent work within an establishment be paid equally, unless the difference is warranted by something other than sex, such as seniority), the Pregnancy Discrimination Amendments to Title VII (which required employers to treat pregnancy as they would other medical conditions), and the Family Medical Leave Act of 1993 (which allows up to twelve weeks of unpaid leave in a given twelve-month period for birth, for

adoption, to care for a family member, or for the employee's own health, and applies only to establishments with more than fifty employees).

23. Hersch, "Employment Discrimination, Economists and the Law."

24. In 1968, for example, the EEOC ruled that sex-segregated help-wanted advertisements in newspapers were illegal, abolishing the practice of newspapers advertising for "male jobs" and "female jobs." The Supreme Court upheld this ruling in 1973.

25. One significant exception lies in the case of single mothers, whose labor force participation rose substantially, by roughly nine percentage points. Government poverty policy changes likely created the driving force behind these increases. The major reform of the welfare system in the mid-1990s made work a condition for receipt of aid and also instituted a five-year lifetime limit, thus changing the program from one of entitlement to a means of temporary assistance. Mosisa and Hipple, "Trends in Labor Force Participation in the United States."

26. Warren and Tyagi, *Two-Income Trap.*

27. Indicators suggest that this recession will produce similar results. Adult women's unemployment rate rose over 2008, but as of November of that year their unemployment rate of 5.5 percent was a full percentage point below the unemployment rate for men. African American women fare worse than white women, with unemployment rates hovering around 9 percent, but still face lower unemployment rates than African American men. Bureau of Labor Statistics, *Economic News Release,* Table A-2.

Two. Why Opting Out Is an Everywoman Issue

1. Wallis, "Case for Staying Home"; Tyson, "What Larry Summers Got Right"; and Yang, "Goodbye to All That."

2. Hirshman, *Get to Work*; Bennetts, *Feminine Mistake.*

3. Cover of *The Feminine Mistake.*

4. Schlafly, "Feminism Is Mugged by Reality."

5. By 2006 the percent had dropped to 70.6 percent. Bureau of Labor Statistics, *Women in the Labor Force: A Databook,* Table 7, p. 18.

6. Cohany and Sok, "Trends in Labor Force Participation of Married Mothers of Infants."

7. As we noted in the previous chapter, historically, black women have worked at higher rates than white women. In 1965, when only 38 percent of white women worked in the paid labor force, almost half of black women did. Black women's participation rates did not rise as steeply as those of white women, and in 2006 black women participated at a rate of 62 percent, only slightly higher than the 59 percent of their white counterparts. Black married mothers also participate at the highest rates of all married mothers. In 2006, three-fourths of black married mothers of children under eighteen participated in the labor force. Non-Hispanic white and Asian married mothers of children under eighteen had similar participation rates of about two-thirds. Hispanic

mothers had the lowest rates, with a labor force participation rate of just over half. Blau, Ferber, and Winkler, *Economics of Women, Men, and Work*, and Bureau of Labor Statistics, *Women in the Labor Force: A Databook 2007*, 10, 15, 16.

8. Boushey, "Opting Out?"

9. Goldin, "Quiet Revolution that Transformed Women's Employment, Education, and Family."

10. MSN.com, "Part-Time Practice Trends Intensify Physician Shortage According to AMGA and Cejka Search 2007 Physician Retention Survey."

11. American Academy of Pediatrics, "Pediatrics Leads Specialties in Number of Part-Time Physicians."

12. Levitt and Venkatesh describe the costs and benefits of using large, nationally representative data sets versus using qualitative data from ethnographic research. Levitt and Venkatesh, "Growing Up in the Projects."

13. We used pseudonyms throughout this book and changed certain identifying details to protect the anonymity of the people who participated in the research for this book.

14. McLaughlin and Kraus, *Nanny Diaries*; Kargman, *Momzillas*.

15. Another example of Upper East Side fiction focusing on this topic is Wolitzer, *Ten-Year Nap*.

16. Cohany and Sok, "Trends in Labor Force Participation of Married Mothers of Infants." These statistics compare the labor force participation of those married mothers of infants who live with an employed husband between 1997 and 2005. Over 52 percent of those whose husband's income put them in the top 20 percent of wage earners were not working in 2005. Interestingly, a similar percent of those in the lowest 20 percent of wage earners also were out of the labor force in 2005.

17. Mason and Ekman, *Mothers on the Fast Track*.

18. Hewlett, Luce, Shiller, and Southwell, "Hidden Brain Drain."

19. Mosisa and Hipple, "Trends in Labor Force Participation in the United States."

20. The U.S. Census Bureau defines stay-at-home fathers to be "married fathers with children younger than fifteen [that] have remained out of the labor force for at least one year primarily so they can care for the family while their wives work outside the home." U.S. Bureau of Census, "Facts for Features. Father's Day: June 15th, 2008"; U.S. Bureau of Census, "Facts for Features. Mother's Day: May 11th, 2008."

21. U.S. Bureau of Census. Survey of Income and Program Participation 2005.

Three. The 100-Hour Couple

An earlier version of a portion of this chapter appeared in *Conformity and Conflict: Readings in Cultural Anthropology*, ed. James Spradley and David McCurdy (New York: Allyn & Bacon, 2009).

1. We adopt a standard cutoff of fifty or more hours per week to indicate whether someone is working extremely long hours. A fifty-hour workweek translates into a ten-hour workday, which can easily turn into eleven hours after commuting.

2. The data from the prior two paragraphs are taken from U.S. Bureau of Census, Current Population Survey, Historical Table A-1.

3. Ramachandran, "Looking for Ms. MBA."

4. At the same time, occupational segregation by gender is alive and well in the United States. If we examine occupational distributions by gender we see that significant differences in the types of jobs held by men and by women still exist. Not surprisingly, the proportions of men and women substantially differ in construction, extraction, and maintenance occupations (17 percent of men, and less than 1 percent of women). And women are overrepresented in office and administrative support jobs (25 percent of women versus 7 percent of men). Fronczek and Johnson, "Occupations: 2000."

5. American Medical Association, Table 1: Physicians by Gender.

6. American Medical Association, Table 16: Physician Specialties by Gender.

7. Commission on Women in the Profession of the American Bar Association, "Current Glance at Women in the Law 2007."

8. National Association for Legal Career Professionals, "Employment Patterns—1982–2004."

9. National Association of Women Lawyers, "National Survey on Retention and Promotion of Women in Law Firms."

10. Salary Wizard.

11. Shellenbarger, "Where Is the Love?"

12. This model is built on the economic theory of international trade between two nations, wherein specialization leads to higher consumption possibilities for both countries.

13. One of the main problems with the specialization of men and women in the traditional marriages of the 1950s was the unequal balance of power within the couples, discussed further in chapter 11. Rose, "Marriage and Assortative Mating."

14. Schwartz and Mare, "Trends in Educational Assortative Marriage from 1940 to 2003."

15. Sweeney and Cancian, "Changing Importance of White Women's Economic Prospects for Assortative Mating."

16. Schor, Overworked American.

17. Jacobs and Gerson, "Who Are the Overworked Americans?"

18. Ibid.

19. Jacobs and Gerson, Time Divide.

20. Kuhn and Lozano, "Expanding Workweek?"

21. Jacobs and Gerson, Time Divide. See also Jacobs and Gerson, "Overworked Individuals or Overworked Families?"

22. Jacobs and Gerson, Time Divide.

23. Since high-earning men are more likely to earn salaries, as opposed to an hourly wage, salaried workers here represent higher-earning workers. Kuhn and Lozano, "Expanding Workweek?"

24. Clark and Oswald, "Satisfaction and Comparison Income."

25. Rivlin, "In Silicon Valley, Millionaires Who Don't Feel Rich."

Four. Glass Ceilings and Maternal Walls

1. According to the Bureau of Labor Statistics, for example, while women now make up the majority of accountants, they earn only 72 percent of what male accountants earn. Female lawyers earn 77 percent of what their male counterparts earn, and female financial managers can expect to earn 62 percent of male earnings. In all management and professional jobs, women earn only 72 percent of what their male counterparts earn. (U.S. Bureau of Labor Statistics, Current Population Survey, Table 39) Women fill just over half of the management and professional occupations, but according to a report by the research organization Catalyst, in 2007 women comprised only 15 percent of Fortune 500 corporate officers and about 7 percent of the top earners, and they held only 15 percent of their board seats. (Catalyst, "2007 Catalyst Census Finds Women Gained Ground as Board Committee Chairs")

2. See Swiss and Walker, *Women and the Work/Family Dilemma*; Still, "Litigating the Maternal Wall"; and Williams and Segal, "Beyond the Maternal Wall."

3. Equal Employment Opportunity Commission, "Charge Statistics."

4. Antilla, *Tales from the Boom-Boom Room.*

5. *Amochaev et al. v. Citigroup Global Markets, Inc.*

6. Selmi, "Sex Discrimination in the Nineties, Seventies Style."

7. *Mercury News*, "Air Force Settles California Gender Bias Suit with Longtime Employee."

8. Pamela Stone, in her study of career women who "opted out" of the workforce, notes a similar absence of discussion of discrimination in the women's narratives. She offers the possibility that while the women may have felt the discrimination, "if they did, they were remarkably resilient in the face of it, and it did not significantly weaken their career attachment." Stone, *Opting Out*, 268.

9. Tannen, *Talking from 9 to 5.*

10. Hewlett, Luce, and Servon, "Stopping the Exodus of Women in Science," 23.

11. Catalyst, *Women in U.S. Corporate Leadership: 2003.* Also see Catalyst, "What Keeps Women from Reaching the Top?"

12. Blau, Ferber, and Winkler, *Economics of Women, Men, and Work*, 215; and Prasso, "Stereotypes about Women Persist in Corporate World."

13. Catalyst, *Women in U.S. Corporate Leadership: 2003.*

14. Catalyst, "Damned or Doomed—Catalyst Study on Gender Stereotyping at Work Uncovers Double-Bind Dilemmas for Women."

15. Forster, "Pregnancy Bias Claims Increase."

16. Feuer, "More Women Accuse Bloomberg Firm of Bias."

17. Equal Employment Opportunity Commission, "Facts about Pregnancy Discrimination."

18. Hananel, "Supreme Court Weighs How Maternity Leave Affects Pensions."

19. Williams, *Unbending Gender*.

20. Gaspar and Glaeser, "Information Technology and the Future of Cities." See also Harford, "Distance Paradox."

21. Uchitelle, "Unsold Homes Tie Down Would-Be Transplants."

22. Jio, "Career Couples Fight over Who's the 'Trailing Spouse.'"

23. Drago and Colbeck, "Final Report for the Mapping Project."

24. Hewlett, Luce, Shiller, and Southwell, "Hidden Brain Drain."

25. Catalyst, *Women in U.S. Corporate Leadership: 2003*.

26. Denise Condon Welsh (Harvard Business School MBA, 1981) as quoted in Blagg and Young, "Redefining Success."

27. Pacenti, "Workplace Discrimination"; and Maschka, "Part-Time Work."

Five. Second Shift Redux

1. Hochschild, with Machung, *Second Shift*.

2. Shellenbarger, "Men Do More Housework than Women Think"; and Sacks, "New Survey Confirms Men Do Fair Share of Household Work."

3. Stratton, "Gains from Trade and Specialization."

4. The source for the statistics in these three paragraphs (except for the information on full-time married mothers, which is cited in the next note) is from the Bureau of Labor Statistics, American Time Use Survey 2006 News Release.

5. Bianchi, Milkie, Sayer, and Robinson, "Is Anyone Doing the Housework?"

6. Hewlett, Luce, Shiller, and Southwell, "Hidden Brain Drain."

7. Keith and Malone, "Housework and the Wages of Young, Middle-Aged, and Older Workers."

8. Greenstein, "Economic Dependence, Gender, and the Division of Labor in the Home."

9. Gupta, "Autonomy, Dependence, or Display?"

10. There is some evidence that shows that women's housework time decreases as her income rises until it matches her husband's income, but that once she begins to outearn him, her housework hours actually begin to rise. In the words of Greenstein, "Breadwinner wives might try to neutralize their deviant economic identity by doing far more housework than might be predicted." Greenstein, "Economic Dependence, Gender, and the Division of Labor in the Home."

11. Stratton, "Why Does More Housework Lower Women's Wages?"

12. Becker, "Human Capital, Effort, and the Sexual Division of Labor."

13. College Nannies and Tutors, "Employing a Nanny."

14. Ehrenreich and Hochschild, *Global Woman*, 2–3.

15. Older Women's League, "Mother's Day Report 2001."

16. Most caregivers are between the ages of eighteen and forty-nine. National Family Caregivers Association, "Caregiving Statistics."

17. Doress-Worters, "Adding Elder Care to Women's Multiple Roles."

18. Pavalko and Henderson, "Combining Care Work and Paid Work."

19. AARP, "Caregiving in the U.S."

20. Pavalko and Henderson, "Combining Care Work and Paid Work."

Six. Child Care Dilemmas

1. "In a survey of 186 cultures around the world, researchers found that older kids, rather than mothers or fathers or other adults, are the primary caretakers of young children." Small, *Kids*, 28.

2. National Association of Child Care Resource and Referral Agencies, "Child Care in America," 1.

3. Kidsdata.org.

4. Linsley, "New Firm Helps Parents in Day Care Search."

5. When available, military-provided child care is ranked among the highest in quality. Gilmore, "DoD Plans to Boost Access to Military Child Care."

6. Nelson, "Childcare Economics Conundrum."

7. This nationally representative study was conducted by researchers at the University of North Carolina at Chapel Hill, the University of Colorado Health Sciences Center, the University of California at Los Angeles, and Yale University.

8. For a detailed description of the rating scales used (the Early Childhood Environmental Rating Scale and the Infant-Toddler Environment Rating Scale) and the results of the Cost, Quality, and Outcomes Study, see Blau, *Childcare Problem*, 41–42.

9. Kontos, Howes, Shinn, and Galinsky, *Quality in Family Child Care and Relative Care*, as cited in Blau, *Childcare Problem*, 43.

10. National Association of Child Care Resource and Referral Agencies, "Child Care in America," 1.

11. National Association of Child Care Resource and Referral Agencies, "Most Recent Child Care Data."

12. University of Minnesota, *2008–2009 Twin Cities Campus Tuition and Fees Reference*.

13. Minnesota Child Care Resource and Referral Network, *2006–2007 Annual Report*.

14. Nocera, "On Day Care, Google Makes a Rare Fumble."

15. Bennetts, *Feminine Mistake*.

16. Blau, *Childcare Problem*.

17. The percent is slightly lower at for-profit centers. Helburn and Howes, "Child Care Cost and Quality."

18. Lefebvre and Merrigan, "Childcare Policy and the Labor Supply of Mothers with Young Children."

19. Grunewald and Rolnick, "Early Childhood Development," 9.

20. Gupta, Smith, and Verner summarize findings from a series of studies on the effect of child care provisions in the Nordic countries. Gupta, Smith, and Verner, "Child Care and Parental Leave in the Nordic Countries."

21. The United States subsidizes child care through a dependent care tax credit and through limited subsidies for low-income parents. Gupta, Smith, and Verner report that the 1995 average annual public subsidy of child care per preschool-age child was roughly $1,800 in the United States, as compared to $8,000 in Denmark and $6,000 in Norway and Sweden.

22. According to the Embassy of France in the United States, almost 100 percent of three- to six-year-olds attend preschool in France, as do roughly 35 percent of two-year-olds. The two-year-olds tend to come from disadvantaged areas.

23. Connelly, DeGraff, and Willis, "Value of Employer-Sponsored Child Care Centers to Employees."

24. McIntyre, "Growth of Work-Site Daycare."

25. Nocera, "On Day Care, Google Makes a Rare Fumble."

26. Ibid.

Seven. Mama Time

The epigraph for this chapter is from the song "Bless My Child," music and lyrics by Dee Carstensen and Julie Dansky. (Skyward Bound Music/BMI Back to Kona/ASCAP), on the album *Can You Hear a Lullaby*, released in 2001. Reprinted by permission of Dee Carstensen.

1. See for example Pamela Stone, who notes: "As a mother myself, I didn't doubt the bit about motherhood and children (at least on my good days)." Stone, *Opting Out*, 3; Leslie Bennetts writes: "I am not criticizing stay-at-home moms for placing the needs of their children ahead of other considerations; I did so myself, and I personally think every member of our society should give top priority to the care and education of our children." Bennetts, *Feminine Mistake*, xxiv.

2. Mason and Ekman, *Mothers on the Fast Track*, 4.

3. Ibid.

4. Gibbs, "Viewpoint."

5. We acknowledge, with gratitude, anthropologist Sonia Patten's insights in helping us frame this issue.

6. St. George, "Despite 'Mommy Guilt,' Time with Kids Increasing."

7. Hays, *Cultural Contradictions of Motherhood*.

8. Baydar, Greek, and Gritz, "Young Mothers' Time Spent at Work and Time Spent Caring for Children."

9. Shapiro, "Keeping Parents Off Campus."

10. Gardner, "In College You Can Go Home Again and Again."

11. St. George, "Despite 'Mommy Guilt,' Time with Kids Increasing."
12. Ibid.
13. YouTube, "Nanny Caught on Tape."

Eight. The Hectic Household

1. Van Gennep, *Rites of Passage.*
2. Bureau of Labor Statistics, "Combined Work Hours Per Week of Husbands and Wives."
3. Go Mom! Schedule, Organize, Grow. See also Web-based family schedule planners, such as the one offered by FamilyCrossings, http://www.familycrossings .com/family_calendar.cfm.
4. Uchitelle, "Unsold Homes Tie Down Would-Be Transplants."
5. Miller, "When Parents Need Their Adult Children."
6. Small, *Kids,* 188.

Nine. The Professionalization of At-Home Motherhood

An earlier version of a portion of this chapter appeared in *Conformity and Conflict: Readings in Cultural Anthropology,* ed. James Spradley and David McCurdy (New York: Allyn & Bacon, 2009).

1. Wells, *Invisible Man.*
2. This idea of the seemingly disempowered asserting their own identity in the face of unrelenting pressures can be seen in other studies of social power, such as Liisa Malkki's *Purity and Exile.*
3. Bennetts, *Feminine Mistake,* and Hirshman, *Get to Work.*
4. *Sex and the City.*
5. Bennetts, *Feminine Mistake.*

Ten. Financial Costs

1. Hewlett, Luce, Shiller, and Southwell, "Hidden Brain Drain."
2. Several reasons come to mind for the wage penalty. Women do not receive on-the-job training while at home, and so their skills may not rise at the same rate as for women who remain in the labor force. In fact, depending on the field, women's skills may even deteriorate while on leave. They also do not build up seniority, and in many cases seniority brings salary increases. Women also are not likely to return to the same job they had before leaving work. If women return to lower-tier jobs, one would expect their salaries to decline.
3. Jacobsen and Levin, "Effects of Intermittent Labor Force Attachment on Women's Earnings."
4. Popenoe and Whitehead, "State of Our Unions."
5. Note here that a college degree per se may not lower the odds of divorce, but rather women who earn college degrees may have certain characteristics that are also conducive to stable marriages.

6. Hurley, "Divorce Rate."

7. High school dropouts are the only group that has experienced rising divorce rates, with a ten-year divorce rate of 46 percent. The data in the next two paragraphs is taken from Popenoe and Whitehead, "State of Our Unions."

8. Popenoe and Whitehead, "State of Our Unions."

9. Heaton, "Factors Contributing to Increased Marital Stability in the United States."

10. While the evidence indicates that cohabitation is more highly associated with divorce, it may be that people who cohabit have different characteristics from those who don't, and it is those characteristics, and not the cohabitation itself, that leads to eventual divorce.

11. Bumpass and Lu, "Trends in Cohabitation and Implications for Children's Family Contexts in the U.S."

12. Ibid.

13. Martin and Parashar, "Women's Changing Attitudes toward Divorce."

14. Peterson, "Re-evaluation of the Economic Consequences of Divorce."

15. Warren and Tyagi, *Two-Income Trap*.

16. Williams, *Unbending Gender*, 115.

17. Arizona, California, Idaho, Louisiana, Nevada, New Mexico, Texas, Washington, and Wisconsin are the nine states with community property laws. Harvard Law Review Association, "Developments in the Law."

18. California, Louisiana, and New Mexico are the three states with community property laws that require a 50–50 split of marital assets. Harvard Law Review Association, "Developments in the Law."

19. Crittenden, *Price of Motherhood*.

20. Williams, *Unbending Gender*, 121, n. 22.

21. GFK Roper Public Affairs and Media, "The Bad News? Child Support and Alimony—Poll Finds Only 25 Percent Receiving All of It."

22. Estin, "Maintenance, Alimony, and the Rehabilitation of Family Care."

23. Dubin, *Prenups for Lovers*.

24. Mahar, "Why Are There So Few Prenuptial Agreements?"

25. Baker and Emery, "When Every Relationship Is Above Average."

26. Mahar, "Why Are There So Few Prenuptial Agreements?"

27. Shidler, "Postnups Becoming New Prenups." The source for the 1980s reference is Felton, "Fastening Your Seatbelt for a Bumpy Marriage."

28. American Academy of Matrimonial Lawyers, "America's Top Divorce Lawyers Cite Postnuptial Agreements as Growing Trend."

29. A *Boston Globe* article tells of a couple who wanted to stay married, but were fighting all the time. He controlled the finances, and she was concerned about what would happen to her financially if they divorced. A mediator suggested a postnup. In it, he put her name on some of the assets and agreed to make payments into an account under her private control. This helped her to relax about the money, and they credit the postnup with saving their marriage. Wen, "Sealing a Contract after the Marriage."

30. Masters, "Postnup Boom among Hedge Fund Managers."

31. Wen, "Sealing a Contract after the Marriage." See also Clement, "Post-Nuptial Agreement Popularity Continues."

32. CNN Money, "Ouch! Don't Forget Disability Insurance."

33. Bernheim, Carman, Gokhale, and Kotlikoff, "Mismatch between Life Insurance Holdings and Financial Vulnerabilities."

34. Bennetts, *Feminine Mistake*.

Eleven. Negotiating without a Paycheck

1. Suppose Lisa likes to cook, but not vacuum, and her husband, Troy, likes to vacuum (he enjoys the lines left on a freshly vacuumed carpet). If Lisa and Troy bargain over household tasks, they likely will assign cooking to Lisa and vacuuming to Troy, thus improving the outcome for both of them.

2. This idea for conceptualizing bargaining is taken from Doss, "Conceptualizing and Measuring Bargaining Power within the Household."

3. Negotiation experts typically measure bargaining power by what they call the "Best Alternative to a Negotiated Agreement" or BATNA.

4. It's called a threat point because that is the point at which she can credibly threaten to leave the marriage.

5. The Urban Dictionary defines "fuck you money" as follows: "any amount of money allowing infinite perpetuation of wealth necessary to maintain a de-sired lifestyle without needing employment or assistance from anyone else."

6. Vora, "Money Doesn't Talk."

7. Ibid.

8. PNC Financial Services Group, Inc., "This Valentine's Day—Give Your Spouse a Budget."

9. McBreen, "Affluent Household Financial Decision-Making."

10. This survey also found that 73 percent of men believe they make most of the financial decisions, while fewer than 50 percent of wives say their husbands are in charge. "Both husbands and wives also tend to attach more importance to their own contributions than their partner does." Regnier and Gengler, "Men, Women . . . and Money."

11. Regnier and Gengler, "Men, Women . . . and Money."

Twelve. Reigniting the Career

1. Mason and Ekman, *Mothers on the Fast Track*.

2. Matthews and Hamilton, "Mean Age of Mother, 1970–2000"; and Martin, Hamilton, Sutton, Ventura, Menacker, Kirmeyer, and Munson, "Births."

3. Bureau of Economic Analysis, National Income and Products Account Tables.

4. Hewlett, Luce, Shiller, and Southwell, "Hidden Brain Drain."

5. Forte Foundation, "Study: Women Who 'Step Out' Hit Wall upon Reentry."

6. Bureau of Labor Statistics, "Average Number of Jobs Started by Individuals from Age 18 to Age 40 in 1978–2004 by Age and Sex."

7. Blau, Ferber, and Winkler, *Economics of Women, Men, and Work*, 279. These numbers are for 2003. The authors get the data from Robert W. Fairlie of the University of California at Santa Cruz, who calculates the numbers from the CPS. Fairlie, "Current Trends in Self-Employed Business Owners by Race."

8. Fairlie includes women self-employed incorporated as well as unincorporated businesses. The Bureau of Labor Statistics restricts the definition of self-employed to unincorporated businesses. Under this measure, female self-employment rates have risen by 25 percent (from 4.4 to 5.5) between 1976 and 2006. Fairlie, "Current Trends in Self-Employed Business Owners by Race."

9. Center for Women's Business Research, "Women-Owned Businesses in the United States, 2006."

10. These categories are defined by the National American Industry Classification System. Real estate includes real estate lessors of residential and nonresidential properties, agents and brokers, property managers, and appraisers. Rental and leasing includes automotive equipment rental and leasing, consumer goods rental, as well as commercial and industrial machinery and equipment rental and leasing.

11. The numbers rise when you include firms with 50 percent women ownership. Center for Women's Business Research, "Women-Owned Businesses in the United States, 2006."

12. Blau, Ferber, and Winkler, *Economics of Women, Men, and Work*, 280; and Ferber and Waldfogel, "'Contingent' Labor Force."

13. Mason and Ekman, *Mothers on the Fast Track*.

14. Hewlett, Luce, Shiller, and Southwell, "Hidden Brain Drain."

15. Shepard and Betof, "Building a Reservoir of Women Superkeepers."

16. Armour, "Moms Find It Easier to Pop Back into the Workforce."

17. Henry, "Comeback Lawyers."

18. American Bar Association, ABA Section of Business Law.

19. Nocera, "On Day Care, Google Makes a Rare Fumble."

20. Nancy Rothbard, as quoted in Knowledge@Wharton, "'Don't Touch My Perks.'"

21. Helfat, "Why a Program on Career Reentry?"

Thirteen. Creative Strategies for Making Work "Work"

1. Cardozo, *Sequencing*.

2. Pew Research Center, "From 1997 to 2007: Fewer Mothers Prefer Full-Time Work."

3. Ibid.

4. American Academy of Pediatrics, "Pediatrics Leads Specialties in Number of Part-Time Physicians."

5. Our research supports a similar finding advanced by Mason and Ekman, *Mothers on the Fast Track*.

6. U.S. Bureau of Census, "Americans Spend More Than 100 Hours Commuting to Work Each Year, Census Bureau Reports."

7. Small, *Kids*, 227–28.

8. Mason and Ekman, *Mothers on the Fast Track.*

Fourteen. Coming of Age in America

1. Roosevelt, *It's Up to the Women.*

2. Belkin, "Looking Back, Moving On."

3. Evans and Grant, *Mama, PhD.*

4. Wagner, *Search for Signs of Intelligent Life in the Universe* (hit Broadway play starring Lily Tomlin, 1985).

5. Aspen Institute Center for Business Education, "Where Will They Lead, 2008."

Bibliography

AARP. Caregiving in the U.S.: Executive Summary." 2004. http://assets.aarp
.org/rgcenter/il/us_caregiving_1.pdf.

American Academy of Matrimonial Lawyers. "America's Top Divorce Lawyers
Cite Postnuptial Agreements as Growing Trend." Press Release, January 31,
2007. http://www.aaml.org/files/public/Postnuptial_Growing_Trend_01
_31_2007.htm.

American Academy of Pediatrics. "Pediatrics Leads Specialties in Number of
Part-Time Physicians." *AAP News*. September 2002. http://www.aap.org/
womenpeds/.

American Bar Association. ABA Section of Business Law. http://www.abanet
.org/dch/committee.cfm?com=CL999500.

American Medical Association. Table 1: Physicians by Gender (excludes students). http://www.ama-assn.org/ama/pub/category/12912.html.

———. Table 16: Physician Specialties by Gender—2006. http://www.ama-assn
.org/ama/pub/category/16229.html.

Amochaev et al. v. Citigroup Global Markets, Inc. D/b/a/ Smith Barney, Case
no. C-05-1298 PJH. http://www.genderlawsuitagainstsmithbarney.com/
press-release-02.htm.

Antilla, Susan. *Tales from the Boom-Boom Room: Women vs. Wall Street.*
Princeton, N.J.: Bloomberg Press, 2002.

Armour, Stephanie. "Moms Find It Easier to Pop Back into the Workforce." *USA
Today*, September 23, 2004. http://www.usatoday.com/money/workplace/
2004-09-23-sequencing_x.htm.

Aspen Institute Center for Business Education. "Where Will They Lead, 2008: MBA
Student Attitudes about Business and Society." April 2008. http://www.aspencbe
.org/documents/ExecutiveSummaryMBAStudentAttitudesReport2008.pdf.

Associated Press. "Air Force Settles California Gender Bias Suit with Longtime
Employee." *Mercury News*, March 6, 2008. http://www.mercurynews.com/
breakingnews/ci_8477378.

Baker, Lynn A., and Robert E. Emery. "When Every Relationship Is above
Average: Perceptions and Expectations for Divorce at the Time of Marriage."
Law and Human Behavior 17, 4 (1993): 439–50.

Baydar, Nazli, April Greek, and R. Mark Gritz. "Young Mothers' Time Spent at Work and Time Spent Caring for Children." *Journal of Family and Economic Issues* 20, 1 (1999): 61–84.

Becker, Gary S. "Human Capital, Effort, and the Sexual Division of Labor." *Journal of Labor Economics* 3 (1985): S33-S58.

Belkin, Lisa. "Looking Back, Moving On." *New York Times*, October 16, 2008, E2.

———. "The Opt-Out Revolution." *New York Times Magazine*, October 26, 2003.

Bennetts, Leslie. *The Feminine Mistake: Are We Giving Up Too Much?* New York: Hyperion, 2007.

Bernheim, Douglas B., Katherine Grace Carman, Jagadeesh Gokhale, and Laurence J. Kotlikoff. "The Mismatch between Life Insurance Holdings and Financial Vulnerabilities: Evidence from the Survey of Consumer Finances." NBER Working Paper no. 8544 (2001).

Bianchi, Suzanne M., Melissa A. Milkie, Liana C. Sayer, and John P. Robinson. "Is Anyone Doing the Housework? Trends in the Gender Division of Household Labor." *Social Forces* 79, 1 (2000): 191–228.

Blagg, Deborah, and Susan Young. "Redefining Success: Women and Work." *Harvard Business School Bulletin*, February 2002. http://www.alumni.hbs .edu/bulletin/2002/february/women.html.

Blau, David M. *The Childcare Problem: An Economic Analysis*. New York: Russell Sage Foundation, 2001.

Blau, Francine D., Marianne A. Ferber, and Anne E. Winkler. *The Economics of Women, Men, and Work*. 5th ed. Upper Saddle River, N.J.: Pearson, Prentice Hall, 2006.

Boushey, Heather. "Opting Out? The Effect of Children on Women's Employment in the United States." *Feminist Economics* 14, 1 (2008): 1–36.

Bumpass, Larry, and Hsien-Hen Lu. "Trends in Cohabitation and Implications for Children's Family Contexts in the U.S." *Population Studies* 54 (2000): 29–41.

Bureau of Economic Analysis. National Income and Products Account Tables. http://www.bea.gov/national/nipaweb/TableView.asp?SelectedTable=1 &ViewSeries=NO&Java=no&Request3Place=N&3Place=N&FromView =YES&Freq=Year&FirstYear=2003&LastYear=2005&3Place=N&Update =Update&JavaBox=no#Mid.

Bureau of Labor Statistics. American Time Use Survey 2006 News Release, Table 8. http://www.bls.gov/news.release/atus.t08.htm.

———. "Average Number of Jobs Started by Individuals from Age 18 to Age 40 in 1978–2004 by Age and Sex." www.bls.gov/nls/y79r21jobsbyage.pdf.

———. "Combined Work Hours Per Week of Husbands and Wives." http:// www.bls.gov/opub/working/page17b.htm.

———. Current Population Survey, Table 39. http://www.bls.gov/cps/#tables.

———. *Databases, Tables, and Calculators*. http://www.bls.gov/#employment.

———. *Databases, Tables, and Calculators*. Historical A Tables. http://www.bls .gov/#employment.

————. *Economic News Release*, Table A-2. http://www.bls.gov/news.release/
empsit.to2.htm.

————. "Employment Projections," Table 3. http://wwwbls.gov/emp/emplabo5
.htm.

————. *Women in the Labor Force: A Databook 2007*, Table 6. http://www.bls
.gov/cps/wlf-databook2007.htm.

Cardozo, Arlene Rossen. *Sequencing: Having It All, But Not All at Once . . .
A New Solution for Women Who Want Marriage, Career, and Family*. New
York: Atheneum Press, 1986.

Catalyst. *Women in U.S. Corporate Leadership: 2003*. New York: Catalyst,
2003.

————. "Damned or Doomed—Catalyst Study on Gender Stereotyping at Work
Uncovers Double-Bind Dilemmas for Women." July 17, 2007. http://www
.catalyst.org/pressroom/pressdoublebind.shtml.

————. "2007 Catalyst Census Finds Women Gained Ground as Board
Committee Chairs." December 10, 2007. http://www.catalyst.org/pressroom/
press_2007_census.shtml.

————. "What Keeps Women from Reaching the Top?" http://www.womens
media.com/new/Catalyst-Women-Executives.shtml.

Center for Women's Business Research. "Women-Owned Businesses in the
United States, 2006: A Fact Sheet." http://www.nfwbo.org.

Clark, Andrew E., and Andrew J. Oswald. "Satisfaction and Comparison
Income." *Journal of Public Economics* 61, 3 (1996): 359–81.

Clement, Daniel. "Post-Nuptial Agreement Popularity Continues." *New
York Divorce Report*, January 14, 2008. http://divorce.clementlaw.com/
2008/01/articles/agreements/post-nuptial-agreements-popularity-
continues/.

CNN Money. "Ouch! Don't Forget Disability Insurance." May 6, 2002. http://
money.cnn.com/2002/03/25/pf/insurance/q_disability/.

Cohany, Sharon, and Emy Sok. "Trends in Labor Force Participation of Married
Mothers of Infants." *Monthly Labor Review* (February 2007): 9–16.

College Nannies and Tutors. "Employing a Nanny: Here Is What You Need
to Know before You Start." http://www.collegenannies.com/nanny/tax
_information.aspx.

Collins, Patricia Hill. *Black Feminist Thought: Knowledge, Consciousness, and
the Politics of Empowerment*. New York: Unwin Hyman, 1990.

Commission on Women in the Profession of the American Bar Association. "A
Current Glance at Women in the Law 2007." http://www.abanet.org/women/
CurrentGlanceStatistics2007.pdf.

Connelly, Rachel, Deborah S. DeGraff, and Rachel Willis. "The Value of
Employer-Sponsored Child Care Centers to Employees." *Industrial Relations*
43, 4 (2004): 759–92.

Coontz, Stephanie. *The Way We Never Were: American Families and the
Nostalgia Trap*. New York: Basic Books, 1992.

Crittenden, Ann. *The Price of Motherhood*. New York: Metropolitan Books, 2001.

Doress-Worters, Paula B. "Adding Elder Care to Women's Multiple Roles: A Critical Review of the Caregiver Stress and Multiple Role Literatures." *Sex Roles: A Journal of Research* 31, 9–10 (1994): 597–614.

Doss, Cheryl. "Conceptualizing and Measuring Bargaining Power within the Household." In *Women, Family, and Work: Writings on the Economics of Gender,* edited by Karine S. Moe, 43–61. Oxford, UK: Blackwell, 2003.

Drago, Robert, and Carol Colbeck. "Final Report for the Mapping Project: Exploring the Terrain of U.S. Colleges and Universities for Faculty and Families." University Park: Pennsylvania State University and the Alfred P. Sloan Foundation, 2003. http://lser.la.psu.edu/workfam/mappingproject .htm.

Dubin, Arlene. *Prenups for Lovers: A Romantic Guide to Prenuptial Agreements.* New York: Random House, 2001.

Ehrenreich, Barbara, and Arlie Hochschild. *Global Woman: Nannies, Maids, and Sex Workers in the New Economy.* New York: Henry Holt, 2004.

Embassy of France in the United States. http://ambafrance-us.org/spip.php ?article555.

Equal Employment Opportunity Commission. "Charge Statistics." http://www .eeoc.gov/stats/charges.html.

———. "Facts about Pregnancy Discrimination." http://www.eeoc.gov/facts/ fs-preg.html.

Estin, Ann Laquer. "Maintenance, Alimony, and the Rehabilitation of Family Care." *North Carolina Law Review* 71 (1993): 721–802.

Evans, Elrena, and Caroline Grant. *Mama, PhD: Women Write about Motherhood and Academic Life.* Piscataway, N.J.: Rutgers University Press, 2008.

Fairlie, Robert W. "Current Trends in Self-Employed Business Owners by Race." Santa Cruz: University of California, 2003. http://people.ucsc.edu/ ~rfairlie/serates/.

Felton, Bruce. "Fastening Your Seatbelt for a Bumpy Marriage." *New York Times,* February 23, 1997. http://query.nytimes.com/gst/fullpage.html?res =9A0CE2DA123EF930A15751C0A961958260.

Ferber, Marianne, and Jane Waldfogel. "The 'Contingent' Labor Force." In *The Elgar Companion to Feminist Economics,* edited by Janice Peterson and Margaret Lewis, 77–82 (Cheltenham, UK: Edward Elgar, 1999.)

Feuer, Alan. "More Women Accuse Bloomberg Firm of Bias." *New York Times,* May 2, 2008.

Flanagan, Caitlan. *To Hell with All That: Loving and Loathing Our Inner Housewife.* New York: Little, Brown, 2006.

Folbre, Nancy. *The Invisible Heart: Economics and Family Values.* New York: New Press, 2001.

Forster, Julie. "Pregnancy Bias Claims Increase." *St. Paul Pioneer Press,* November 6, 2008, 3A, 3C.

Forte Foundation. "Study: Women Who 'Step Out' Hit Wall Upon Reentry." Press Release, July 15, 2005. http://www.fortefoundation.org/site/DocServer/ BackintheGame.pdf?docID=4022.

Fronczek, Peter, and Patricia Johnson. "Occupations: 2000." *Census 2000 Brief*, C2KBR-25, August 2003. http://www.census.gov/prod/2003pubs/ c2kbr-25.pdf.

Gardner, Ralph, Jr. "In College You Can Go Home Again and Again." *New York Times*, December 14, 2006.

Gaspar, Jess, and Edward L. Glaeser. "Information Technology and the Future of Cities." *Journal of Urban Economics* 43, 1 (January 1998): 136–56.

GFK Roper Public Affairs and Media. "The Bad News? Child Support and Alimony—Poll Finds Only 25 Percent Receiving All of It." *PR Newswire*, January 17, 2006. http://www.breitbart.com/print.php?id=prnw.20080117 .CLTH085&show_article=1&catnum=7.

Gibbs, Nancy. "Viewpoint: Bring On the Daddy Wars," *Time*, February 27, 2006. http://www.time.com/time/nation/article/0,8599,1168125,00.html.

Gilmore, Gerry J. "DoD Plans to Boost Access to Military Child Care." *American Forces Press Service News Articles*. Jan. 26, 2006. http://www.defenselink .mil/news/newsarticle.aspx?id=14518.

Go Mom! Schedule, Organize, Grow. http://www.gomominc.com/solutions/ newyear.html.

Goldin, Claudia. "The Quiet Revolution that Transformed Women's Employment, Education, and Family." *American Economic Review* 96, 2 (2006): 1–21.

———. *Understanding the Gender Gap: An Economic History of American Women*. Oxford: Oxford University Press, 1990.

Greenstein, Theodore N. "Economic Dependence, Gender, and the Division of Labor in the Home: A Replication and Extension." *Journal of Marriage and the Family* 62, 2 (2000): 322–35.

Grunewald, Rob, and Arthur Rolnick. "Early Childhood Development: Economic Development with a High Public Return." *Region* 17, 4, Supplement (December 2003): 9.

"Guide to Hiring Women." *Transportation* magazine, 1943. Reproduced in *Savvy and Sage*, October 2007.

Gupta, Nabanita Datta, Nina Smith, and Mette Verner. "Child Care and Parental Leave in the Nordic Countries: A Model to Aspire To?" IZA Discussion Paper no. 2014, 2006.

Gupta, Sanjiv. "Autonomy, Dependence, or Display? The Relationship between Married Women's Earnings and Housework." *Journal of Marriage and the Family* 69 (2007): 399–417.

Hananel, Sam. "Supreme Court Weighs How Maternity Leave Affects Pensions." *Associated Press*, December 11, 2008, downloaded from the *United States Supreme Court Monitor*, http://www.law.com/jsp/scm/PubArticleSCM.jsp ?id=1202426653329.

Harford, Tim. "The Distance Paradox: If Telecommuting Is So Easy, Why Do

We Travel for Work More Than Ever?" *Slate*, February 3, 2007. http://www.slate.com/id/2158571.

Harvard Law Review Association. "Developments in the Law: The Law of Marriage and the Family." *Harvard Law Review* 116, 7 (2003): 1996–2122.

Hays, Sharon. *The Cultural Contradictions of Motherhood*. London: Yale University Press, 1998.

Heaton, Tim B. "Factors Contributing to Increased Marital Stability in the United States." *Journal of Family Issues* 23, 3 (2002): 392–409.

Helburn, Suzanne W., and Carollee Howes. "Child Care Cost and Quality." *The Future of Children* 6, 2 (Summer/Fall 1996): 62–82.

Helfat, Constant E. "Why a Program on Career Reentry? Tuck School Back in Business Program." July 5, 2006. www.tuck.dartmouth.edu/exec/pdf/bib_helfat_speech.pdf.

Henry, Deborah Epstein. "Comeback Lawyers: A Look at Why Re-Entry is a Hot Work/Life Balance Topic." *Diversity & the Bar* (January/February 2007). http://www.flextimelawyers.com/pdf/art11.pdf.

Hersch, Joni. "Employment Discrimination, Economists and the Law." In *Women, Family and Work: Writings on the Economics of Gender*, edited by Karine S. Moe, 217–33. Oxford, UK: Blackwell, 2003.

Hewlett, Sylvia Ann, Carolyn Buck Luce, and Lisa J. Servon. "Stopping the Exodus of Women in Science." *Harvard Business Review* 86, 6 (2008): 22–24.

Hewlett, Sylvia Ann, Carolyn Buck Luce, Peggy Shiller, and Sandra Southwell. "The Hidden Brain Drain: Off-ramps and On-ramps in Women's Careers." *Harvard Business Review Research Report* (March 2005).

Hirshman, Linda R. *Get to Work: A Manifesto for Women of the World*. New York: Viking Press, 2006.

Hochschild, Arlie Russell, with Anne Machung. *The Second Shift: Working Parents and the Revolution at Home*. New York: Viking Press, 1989.

Hurley, Dan. "Divorce Rate: It's Not As High As You Think." *New York Times*, April 19, 2005.

Jacobs, Jerry A., and Kathleen Gerson. "Overworked Individuals or Overworked Families? Explaining Trends in Work, Leisure, and Family Time." *Work and Occupations* 28, 1 (2001): 40–63.

———. *The Time Divide*. Cambridge, Mass.: Harvard University Press, 2004.

———. "Who Are the Overworked Americans?" *Review of Social Economy* 56 (1998): 442–59.

Jacobsen, Joyce P., and Laurence M. Levin. "Effects of Intermittent Labor Force Attachment on Women's Earnings," *Monthly Labor Review* 118, 9 (1995): 14–19.

Jio, Sarah. "Career Couples Fight over Who's the Trailing Spouse." *New York Times*, June 26, 2008.

Kargman, Jill. *Momzillas*. New York: Broadway Publishers and McLaughlin, 2007.

Keith, Kristen, and Paula Malone. "Housework and the Wages of Young, Middle-Aged, and Older Workers." *Contemporary Economic Policy* 23, 2 (2005): 224–41.

Kidsdata.org. http://www.kidsdata.org/topictrends.jsp?csid=0&t=40&i=3&ra =3_132&link=.

Knowledge@Wharton. "'Don't Touch My Perks': Companies that Eliminate Them Risk Employee Backlash." July 23, 2008. http://knowledge.wharton .upenn.edu/article.cfm?articleid=2019.

Kontos, Susan, Carollee Howes, Marybeth Shinn, and Ellen Galinsky. *Quality in Family Child Care and Relative Care.* New York: Teachers College Press, 1995, cited in David M. Blau, *The Childcare Problem: An Economic Analysis.* (New York: Russell Sage Foundation, 2001.)

Kuhn, Peter, and Fernando Lozano. "The Expanding Workweek? Understanding Trends in Long Work Hours Among U.S. Men, 1979–2004. NBER Working Paper no. 11895. December 2005.

Lefebvre, Pierre, and Philip Merrigan. "Childcare Policy and the Labor Supply of Mothers with Young Children: A Natural Experiment from Canada." *Journal of Labor Economics* 23, 3 (2008): 519–48.

Levitt, Steven, and Sudhir Alladia Venkatesh. "Growing Up in the Projects: The Economic Lives of a Cohort of Men Who Came of Age in Chicago Public Housing." *American Economic Review* 91, 2 (2001): 79–84.

Linsley, Jeanne. "New Firm Helps Parents in Day Care Search." Career/Life Alliance Services. http://www.clalliance.net/worklife/en/newfirm.asp.

Mahar, Heather. "Why Are There So Few Prenuptial Agreements?" John M. Olin Center for Law, Economics and Business Discussion Paper Series no. 423. Harvard Law School, 2003. http://lsr.nellco.org/harvard/olin/papers/436.

Malkki, Liisa. *Purity and Exile: Violence, Memory, and National Cosmology Among Hutu Refugees in Tanzania.* Chicago: University of Chicago Press, 1995.

Martin, Joyce A., Brady E. Hamilton, Paul D. Sutton, Stephanie J. Ventura, Fay Menacker, Sharon Kirmeyer, and Martha L. Munson. "Births: Final Data for 2005." *National Vital Statistics Reports* 56, 6 (December 5, 2007).

Martin, Steven P., and Sangeeta Parashar. "Women's Changing Attitudes toward Divorce: 1974–2002: Evidence for an Educational Crossover." *Journal of Marriage and Family* 68, 1 (2006): 29–40.

Maschka, Kristin. "Part-Time Work: What's So Lucky About It?" Mothers & More, http://www.mothersandmore.org/Advocacy/PartTimeWork.shtml.

Mason, Mary Ann, and Eve Mason Ekman. *Mothers on the Fast Track: How a New Generation Can Balance Family and Careers.* New York: Oxford University Press, 2007.

Masters, Brooke. "Postnup Boom among Hedge Fund Managers." *Financial Times*, May 30, 2007. http://us.ft.com/ftgateway/superpage.ft?news_id =ft005302007172678254.

Matthews, T. J., and Brady E. Hamilton. "Mean Age of Mother, 1970–2000." *National Vital Statistics Report* 51, 1 (December 11, 2002).

McBreen, Catherine. "Affluent Household Financial Decision-Making." *Spectrem Perspective Report*. Interview by Farrell Kramer (Podcast), 8 min., 39 sec., Farrell Kramer Communications, http://www.millionairecorner.com/index.php/Affluent-Insights-Podcasts/LISTEN-Affluent-Household-Financial-Decision-Making.html.

McIntyre, Lee. "The Growth of Work-Site Daycare." *Regional Review: The Federal Reserve Bank of Boston* 10, 3 (2000): 8–15.

McLaughlin, Emma, and Nicola Kraus. *The Nanny Diaries: A Novel*. New York: St. Martin's Press, 2002.

Mercury News. "Air Force Settles California Gender Bias Suit with Longtime Employee." March 6, 2008. http://www.mercurynews.com/breakingnews/ci_8477378.

Miller, Julie. "When Parents Need Their Adult Children." *New York Times*, August 4, 1996.

Minnesota Child Care Resource and Referral Network. *2006–2007 Annual Report*. http://www.mnchildcare.org/mktg_matls/2007_Annual.pdf.

Mom Corps. http://www.momcorps.com.

Mosisa, Abraham, and Steven Hipple. "Trends in Labor Force Participation in the United States." *Monthly Labor Review* 129, 10 (October 2006): 35–57.

MSN.com. *Part-Time Practice Trends Intensify Physician Shortage According to AMGA and Cejka Search 2007 Physician Retention Survey*. PRNewswire, March 10, 2008.http://www.reuters.com/article/pressRelease/idUS134560+10-Mar-2008+PRN20080310.

National Association for Legal Career Professionals. "Employment Patterns—1982–2004." http://www.nalp.org/content/index.php?pid=385.

National Association of Child Care Resource and Referral Agencies. "Child Care in America: 2008 State Fact Sheets." http://www.naccrra.org/policy/docs/ChildCareinAmerica.pdf.

———. "Most Recent Child Care Data: State by State." http://www.naccrra.org/randd/state_by_state_facts.php.

National Association of Women Lawyers. "National Survey on Retention and Promotion of Women in Law Firms." November 2007. http://www.abanet.org/nawl/docs/FINAL_survey_report_11-14-07.pdf.

National Family Caregivers Association. "Caregiving Statistics: Statistics on Family Caregivers and Family Caregiving." http://www.nfcacares.org/who_are_family_caregivers/care_giving_statstics.cfm.

Nelson, Julie. "The Childcare Economics Conundrum: Quality versus Affordability." In *Women, Family, and Work: Writings on the Economics of Gender*, edited by Karine S. Moe, 125–41. Oxford, UK: Blackwell, 2003.

Nocera, Joe. "On Day Care, Google Makes a Rare Fumble." *New York Times*, July 5, 2008.

Older Women's League. "Mother's Day Report 2001: Faces of Caregiving." http://www.owl-national.org/Mothers_Day_Reports.html.

On-Ramps Services LLC. http://www.on-ramps.com.

Pacenti, John. "Workplace Discrimination: Hitting the 'Maternal Wall.'"

Daily Business Review, January 24, 2008. http://www.law.com/jsp/ihc/PubArticleIHC.jsp?id=1201255554661.

Pavalko, Eliza K., and Kathryn A. Henderson. "Combining Care Work and Paid Work: Do Workplace Policies Make a Difference?" Research on Aging 28, 3 (May 2006): 359–74.

Peterson, Richard R. "A Re-Evaluation of the Economic Consequences of Divorce." American Sociological Review 61, 3 (1996): 528–36.

Pew Research Center. "From 1997 to 2007: Fewer Mothers Prefer Full-time Work." PewResearchCenter: A Social and Demographic Trends Report (July 12, 2007). http://pewresearch.org/pubs/536/working-women.

PNC Financial Services Group, Inc. "This Valentine's Day—Give Your Spouse a Budget . . . It Might Save Your Marriage. PNC Finds Women and Men Divided Over Finances, and Recommends a Financial Partnership to Strengthen the Relationship." PRNewswire, February 9, 2006. www.harrisinteractive.com/services/pubs/PNC_Give_Your_Spouse_a_Budget.pdf.

Popenoe, David, and Barbara Dafoe Whitehead. "The State of Our Unions: The Social Health of Marriage in America 2007." National Marriage Project at Rutgers, the State University of New Jersey. http://marriage.rutgers.edu/Publications/SOOU/TEXTSOOU2007.htm.

Prasso, Sheri. "Stereotypes about Women Persist in Corporate World." Associated Press, Business News, February 27, 1996.

Ramachandran, Nisha. "Looking for Ms. MBA." U.S. News and World Report, February 15, 2008.

Regnier, Pat, and Amanda Gengler. "Men, Women . . . and Money." Money, March 14, 2006. http://money.cnn.com/2006/03/10/pf/marriagemain_moneymag_0604/index.htm.

Rivlin, Gary. "In Silicon Valley, Millionaires Who Don't Feel Rich." New York Times, August 5, 2007. http://www.nytimes.com/2007/08/05/technology/05rich.html?ei=5088&emc=rss&en=003719e2d0560842&ex=1343966400&partner=rssnyt.

Roosevelt, Anna Eleanor. It's Up to the Women. New York: Frederick A. Stokes Co., 1933.

Rose, Elaina. "Marriage and Assortative Mating: How Have the Patterns Changed?" Working Paper no. 22, Center for Statistics and the Social Science, University of Washington, December 2001.

Sacks, Glenn. "New Survey Confirms Men Do Fair Share of Household Work." Pasadena Star-News and Affiliated Papers, April 7, 2002. http://www.glennsacks.com/new_survey_confirms.htm.

Salary Wizard. http://www.salary.com.

Schlafly, Phyllis. "Feminism Is Mugged by Reality." Phyllis Schlafly Report 38, 5 (December 2004). http://www.eagleforum.org/psr/2004/dec04/psrdec04.html.

Schor, Juliet. The Overworked American: The Unexpected Decline of Leisure. New York: Basic Books, 1991.

Schwartz, Christine R., and Robert D. Mare. "Trends in Educational Assortative

Marriage from 1940 to 2003." *Demography* 42, 4 (November 2005): 621–46.

Selmi, Michael. "Sex Discrimination in the Nineties, Seventies Style: Case Studies in the Preservation of Male Workplace Norms." Working Paper no. 73, George Washington University Public Law and Legal Theory, 2003.

Seuss, Dr. *Oh, the Places You'll Go!* New York: Random House, 1990.

Sex and the City. "Time and Punishment" (episode 55, season 4), 1998.

Shapiro, Judith. "Keeping Parents off Campus." *New York Times*, August 22, 2002.

Shellenbarger, Sue. "Men Do More Housework Than Women Think." *Wall Street Journal Online*, May 20, 2005. http://careerpath.org/columnists/workfamily/20050520-workfamily.html.

———. "Where Is the Love? Students Eschew Campus Romance." *Wall Street Journal*, January 31, 2008.

Shepard, Molly Dickinson, and Nila G. Betof. "Building a Reservoir of Women Superkeepers." In *The Talent Management Handbook: Creating Organizational Excellence by Identifying, Developing, and Promoting Your Best People*, edited by Lance A. Berger and Dorothy Berger, 279–90. New York: McGraw-Hill, 2003.

Shidler, Lisa. "Postnups Becoming New Prenups." *InvestmentNews*, June 18, 2007. http://www.investmentnews.com/apps/pbcs.dll/article?AID=/20070618/FREE/70618002.

Small, Meredith F. *Kids: How Biology and Culture Shape the Way We Raise Our Children.* New York: Doubleday, 2001.

St. George, Donna. "Despite 'Mommy Guilt,' Time with Kids Increasing; Society's Pressures, Own Expectations Alter Priorities." *Washington Post*, March 20, 2007.

Still, Mary C. "Litigating the Maternal Wall: U.S. Lawsuits Charging Discrimination against Workers with Family Responsibilities." Center for WorkLife Law, University of California Hastings College of Law. July 6, 2006. http://www.worklifelaw.org/pubs/FRDreport.pdf.

Stone, Pamela. *Opting Out: Why Women Really Quit Careers and Head Home.* Berkeley: University of California Press, 2007.

Stratton, Leslie. "Gains from Trade and Specialization: The Division of Work in Married Couple Households." In *Women, Family, and Work: Writings on the Economics of Gender*, edited by Karine S. Moe, 67–83. Oxford, UK: Blackwell, 2003.

———. "Why Does More Housework Lower Women's Wages?: Testing Hypotheses Involving Job Effort and Hours Flexibility." *Social Science Quarterly* 82, 1 (2001): 67–76.

Sweeney, Megan M., and Maria Cancian. "Changing Importance of White Women's Economic Prospects for Assortative Mating." *Journal of Marriage and Family* 66, 4 (November 2004): 1015–28.

Swiss, Deborah J., and Judith P. Walker. *Women and the Work/Family*

Dilemma: How Today's Professional Women Are Confronting the Maternal Wall. New York: John Wiley and Sons, 1994.

Tannen, Deborah. *Talking from 9 to 5.* New York: Harper Collins, 1994.

Tuck School of Business at Dartmouth College. "Back in Business: Invest in Your Return." http://www.tuck.dartmouth.edu/exec/targeted_audiences/back_in _business.html#goals.

Tyson, Laura D'Andrea. "What Larry Summers Got Right." *Business Week,* March 28, 2005.

Uchitelle, Louis. "Unsold Homes Tie Down Would-Be Transplants." *New York Times,* April 3, 2008.

University of Minnesota. *2008–2009 Twin Cities Campus Tuition and Fees Reference.* http://onestop.umn.edu/finances/costs_and_tuition/tuition_and _fees/index.html.

Urban Dictionary. "fuck you money." http://www.urbandictionary.com/define .php?term=fuck+you+money.

U.S. Bureau of the Census. Bureau News. "Americans Spend More Than 100 Hours Commuting to Work Each Year, Census Bureau Reports." March 30, 2005. http://www.census.gov/Press-Release/www/releases/archives/american _community_survey_acs/004489.html.

———. CPS Databases, 2008, Table A-2. http://www.bls.gov/news.release/empsit .t02.htm.

———. Current Population Survey. Historical Table A-1. http://www.census.gov/ population/www/socdemo/educ-attn.html.

———. "Facts for Features. Father's Day: June 15, 2008." April 17, 2008. http:// www.census.gov/Press-Release/www/releases/archives/facts_for_features _special_editions/011778.html.

———. "Facts for Features. Mother's Day: May 11, 2008." March 13, 2008. http:// www.census.gov/Press-Release/www/releases/archives/facts_for_features _special_editions/011633.html.

———. Survey of Income and Program Participation 2005, Historical Table. http://www.census.gov/population/www/socdemo/childcare.html.

———. *2008 Statistical Abstract of the United States.*

U.S. Department of Agriculture. *Expenditures on Children by Families, 2007.* Miscellaneous Publication no. 1528.

Van Gennep, Arnold. *The Rites of Passage.* 1908. Reprint, Chicago: University of Chicago Press, 1960.

Van Horn, Carl E., and Herbert A. Schaffner. *Work in America: An Encyclopedia of History, Policy, and Society.* Santa Barbara: ABC-CLIO, 2003.

Vora, Shivani. "Money Doesn't Talk." *New York Times,* January 14, 2007.

Wagner, Jane. *The Search for Signs of Intelligent Life in the Universe.* Play performed on Broadway, 1985.

Wallis, Claudia. "The Case for Staying Home." *Time* 163, 12 (March 2004).

Warren, Elizabeth, and Amelia Warren Tyagi. *The Two-Income Trap.* New York: Basic Books, 2003.

Wells, H. G. *The Invisible Man*. UK: C. Arthur Pearson, 1987.

Wen, Patricia. "Sealing a Contract after the Marriage." *Boston Globe*, December 19, 2005. http://www.boston.com/yourlife/relationships/articles/2005/12/19/sealing_a_contract_after_the_marriage/.

Williams, Joan. *Unbending Gender: Why Work and Family Conflict and What to Do About It*. New York: Oxford University Press, 1999.

Williams, Joan, and Nancy Segal. "Beyond the Maternal Wall: Relief for Family Caregivers Who Are Discriminated against on the Job." *Harvard Women's Law Review* 26 (2003): 77–162.

Wolitzer, Meg. *The Ten-Year Nap*. New York: Riverhead Press, 2008.

Yang, Jia. "Goodbye to All That." *Fortune* 152, 10 (November 14, 2005): 169–70.

YouTube. "Nanny Caught on Tape." 2 min., 20 sec. www.youtube.com/watch?v=S2iDTpiiiEU.

Index

ers: appeal of, 165–66; breaks from, 27, 112, 147; and caregiving, 68–70, 95, 106; and hectic household, 100; and housework, 62–64; personal experience, ix; return to, 151, 155–56; and self-employment, 153, 171; shifts in, 2–3, 14; telecommuting, 163, 169; and travel, 104

Full-time motherhood, ix, 28, 85, 95, 104, 121, 126

Gender division of labor, 7, 61, 68, 72, 89, 92, 111

Gender gap. *See* Education; Income; Labor force participation; Work hours

Gerson, Kathleen, 42

Glass ceilings, 6–7, 45–46, 48–53, 58, 176. *See also* Discrimination

Globalization, 43, 55, 67, 103

Goldin, Claudia, 13, 18, 24–27

Harvard University, 94, 119, 143, 160, 193nn17–18

Health: child care provider, 67, 93, 98, 103, 105; and sick child, x, 82, 94–95, 98, 105, 168. *See also* Elderly care

Health care, 34, 68–69, 147

Health insurance. *See* Insurance

Hochschild, Arlie, 61–62, 67

Household help, 7, 44, 61–62, 66, 87, 95, 176

Households: *See* Bargaining power; Housework: division of, in households

Housework: division of, in households, 7, 61–66, 69–70; gendered nature of, 64–65; hours spent on, 63–64; outsourcing of, 66–67; to promote husband's career, 111, 124, 143; societal role in determining, 67–68; and technological changes, 17–18; and women's

wages, 65–66. *See also* "Second shift"

Human capital. *See* Education; Skills

Identity, xi, 2, 4, 23, 34, 72, 85, 88, 126, 177, 189n10; cultural definitions of, 72; and empowerment, 192n2 (chap. 9); occupation as source of, 6, 114–15, strategies for maintaining, 118–20

Income, 2, 13, 14, 16, 28, 29, 30, 39–40, 90, 118, 186n16; and child care 73–74, 78–80, 96, 191n21; and decision making in households, 145–46; and divorce outcomes, 130, 132, 133; and financial independence 8, 29, 108, 135, 141–42, 144, 147–48; and hours worked, 4, 41–43, 100, 175; and housework, 65, 189n10; of men versus women, 35, 45, 56, 188n1; penalties for opting out, 9, 79, 127–28, 132, 179, 192n2 (chap. 10); replacement (*see* Insurance); rise in women's, 4, 17, 18, 66

Insurance, 66, 146; disability, 136; health, 154; life, 137

Jacobs, Jerry, 42

Job transfer, 56–58, 105, 107, 169

Kindergarten, 81

Kuhn, Peter, 42–43, 188n23

Labor, Department of, 81

Labor force participation: of African American women, 12, 184n13, 185n7; differences in, by class, 13–16; explanation of trends in, 16–19; and family balance, 4, 165–67; of married women, 2, 3, 11–16, 19–20, 22–24, 27, 183n1 (chap.1), 185n16; of men versus women, 11–12

Law, 184n22; attitudes of, toward divorce, 131; for determining child support (see Child support); for division of assets following divorce, 132–33, 193nn17–18; Pregnancy Discrimination Act of 1979, 54; Uniform Marriage and Divorce Act, 133–34. See also Civil Rights Act of 1964, Title VII; Discrimination; Divorce: and prenuptial and postnuptial agreements; Equal Employment Opportunity Commission; Postnuptial Agreements
Law firms, 38, 107, 157, 165
Law schools, 35, 37–38, 152
Lawsuits, 47, 54
Lawyers: American Academy of Matrimonial, 135; and American Bar Association, 157; career dissatisfaction of, 31–32, 90; compensation of, 38, 188n1; divorce, 135; part-time, 59, 107, 161, 165–66; wage penalty for women, 128; women, in the judiciary, 37; women's representation as, 37–38, 157
Leisure, 39, 40, 64, 78
Love, 38, 83, 99, 139, 142, 144; of job, 48, 57, 70, 93, 143, 169
Lozano, Fernando, 42–43, 188n23

Managers, 9, 37, 39, 42, 43, 53–55, 59, 68, 116, 150, 175, 188n1
Marriage, 8, 13, 18, 38, 175; and assortative mating, 39, 44, 187n13; bargaining within (see Bargaining power); and education level, 129–31; and employment status 13, 23, 28, 39 (see also Labor force participation); and housework (see Housework); marriage bars, 14, 19; and prenuptial and postnuptial agreements (see under Divorce)

Maternal walls, 6–7, 45–46, 48, 52–60, 176; faced by men, 60
Maternity leave, 53–54, 75, 77, 158; and Family Medical Leave Act of 1993, 184n22; and Pregnancy Discrimination Act of 1979, 54. See also Parental leave
MBAS, 31, 94, 119, 143, 160, 173, 181
Mead, Margaret, 84
Medical doctors. See Physicians
Medical problems. See Health
Medical schools, 25, 37, 90, 153
Men: compared with women, 4, 45, 48, 56, 58, 167, 173, 175–76, 179, 184n22, 185n27; dependency of women on, 21; and divorce, 132–36; education of, 36–37, 160; and financial decision making, 145–46, 194n10; and hours worked, 40–43, 188n23; and household responsibilities, 62–65, 69–70; and ideal worker, 54, 176; and male culture at work, 49–52; and marriage markets, 39–40, 130; opting out, 32–33, 117; and parenting, 60, 88–89, 92; in the workforce, 9, 11, 14–15, 18, 37, 82, 156–58, 165, 182
Middle-class 4, 13, 15, 16, 28, 110
Millennial, 180–82
"Mommy guilt," 172
"Mommy time," 4, 110
"Mommy track," 5–7, 52
"Mommy wars," xi, 89, 125
Mothers, division among. See "Mommy wars"
Mothers, employed. See Working mothers
Mothers, stay-at-home. See Stay-at-home mothers

Nanny: cams, 94; and career success, 53, 172; covering for sick,

in, over time, 40, 41, 102; expectations regarding, 6–7, 43, 55; in household (see Housework); and income (see Income); men's, 33, 41–43; reductions in, as strategy, 4, 25, 27, 35, 40, 99, 112, 122, 163–66; of women versus men, 40, 42

Working mothers: attitudes toward, 6, 13–15, 84 (see also "Mommy wars"; Stereotypes); and child care usage, 73–74, 77, 81–82; and full-time versus part-time ideal, 165; and leisure, 64, 78; and time spent with children, 91; and wage gap with childless women, 45. See also Bias avoidance; Full-time employment, of mothers; Labor force participation; Part-time employment

Yard work, 64–66

CPSIA information can be obtained
at www.ICGtesting.com
Printed in the USA
LVOW03s2223231217
560712LV00001B/59/P

9 780820 334042